ROOTED & GROUNDED

in *Christ*

DR. BRIDGET SHEMWELL

Printed in the United States of America

Master Group 2019

Cover design and illustration: Dylan Drake, www.dylandrakedesigninc.com

ISBN 978-0-9600705-0-3

To my dear friend, Suzanne,
for planting the seed in my heart
to work out my own salvation.

"I have fought the good fight, I have finished the race,
I have kept the faith.
Now there is in store for me the crown of righteousness,
which the Lord, the righteous Judge, will award to me
on that day—and not only to me,
but also to all who have longed for his appearing."

2 Timothy 4:7 – 8 (NIV)

Let's not get tired of *doing what is good.* At just the right time we will *Reap a harvest of* *Blessing* if we don't give up.

Galatians 6:9 (NLT)

ACKNOWLEDGMENTS

I would like to thank my Lord and Savior Jesus Christ for giving me the daily strength and courage to write this book and share my own freedom story. I would like to thank my husband, Jim, for his loving encouragement and support. Thank you to our boys, Zack, Vince, and Dobie Max for bringing so much energy and joy into our lives. Thanks to my parents for teaching me the value of hard work. I love you very much. To my siblings, Bill and Sheri, I always hold you tenderly and close to my heart. Thank you to my grandmothers on both sides for being Christ-centered and the solid foundation of our family. Special thanks to Dr. Brenda Randle and my colleague and prayer partner Dr. Blanche Hunt. Lastly, thanks to Christian authors, Sharon Jaynes and Rebekah Lyons. Their books have inspired and encouraged me throughout this writing process.

Unless otherwise indicated, all Scripture quotations are taken from the Holy Bible, New International Version, NIV. Copyright 1973, 1978, 1984, 2011, by Biblica, Inc.

For **God is working in you,** giving you the desire and power to **do what pleases him.**

Philippians 2:13 (NLT)

PREFACE

Even though I accepted Jesus Christ as my Savior at the age of 12, my faith was kept hidden from others as I continued to indulge in habitual sins during my teenage, early and mid-adult years. I feel like God has been waiting 30 years for me to love Him *with all my heart, with all my soul, with all my mind, and with all my strength.*

The problem was I did not know *how* to love and have a relationship with Christ. I imagine there are others, like myself, who accepted Jesus but maybe did not have an example or a role model to mentor them in their Christian walk and teach them how to *grow* in their salvation. If so, this book is for you.

In *Rooted & Grounded in Christ*, you will understand how Satan uses *thorns* (habitual sins) against you and me as strongholds to hinder us from having a personal relationship with Jesus. Through Paul's prison letters, you will recognize how to be set free from the bondage of habitual sins by trusting God, having faith in Jesus, and accessing the resurrection power that lives inside of you. Jesus desires to have a relationship with you and His bride, the Church. From Paul's letters to the churches at Ephesus, Colossae, and Philippi, you will discover your true identity in Christ, how to develop an intimate relationship with Him, and how to thrive in the fullness and abundance of God's love for you.

Paul's letters from prison plant the foundational seeds for being rooted in love, grounded in Christ, and growing in the fullness of God through the Holy Spirit from salvation into sanctification. First, you will understand the **Mystery of God** as you pursue Jesus with a **pure heart** to help you overcome the habitual sins of the old self.

Rooted in Love, *Grounded* in Christ, and *Growing* in the Fullness of *God*

Glory of God
Prosper
Soul

Promises of God
Persevere
Strength

Armor of God
Protect
Mind

Mystery of God
Pure
Heart

Justification

Transformation

Application

Sanctification

Next, you will learn how to put on the full **Armor of God** to transform and **protect** your **mind** by replacing old habits with new ones. Then, as you apply these new habits, you will know how to **persevere** in the **strength** and power of Jesus and claim the **Promises of God**. As you reap these fundamental truths, you will experience spiritual discernment, wisdom, and mature in the fullness and **Glory of God**.

At each new level, your **soul** will **prosper** as you sow the seeds of faith, abide in Jesus, and walk in forgiveness and true freedom. As believers, we are called to take this freedom and serve one another in love. The benefits we reap from serving and abiding in His righteousness lead to bearing fruit for God's harvest. As you read and discover, the reward is abundant living on earth and eternal life with Him in heaven.

HOW TO USE THIS BIBLE STUDY

This Bible study is interactive and designed for individuals, small, or large groups to use over a five-week period. However, I encourage you to read and use this Bible study at your own pace. The study intends to draw the reader into exploring and reflecting on the daily readings and activities located in the *Rooted: Growing in Christ – Workbook* (optional).

Participants are provided a **Reader's Guide**, located in the appendix of this book, to expand the weekly lessons for those interested in an in-depth Bible study based on specific passages of Scripture. The **Reader Guide** has background information on **God's Covenants, The Christian Movement, and The Missionary Journeys of Paul**.

The Bible study along with the workbook activities will give you an opportunity to (re)discover and share with others your journey into freedom and abundant living. My prayer for you is to grow and abide in the knowledge of the true vine, the courage to bear fruit for His Kingdom, and the wisdom to follow God's two greatest commandments. The first one is to *"**Love the Lord your God** with all your **heart** and with all your **soul** and with all your **mind**, and with all your **strength**.* The second is this: '**Love** your neighbor as yourself.' There is no commandment greater than these" (*Mark 12:30 – 31*).

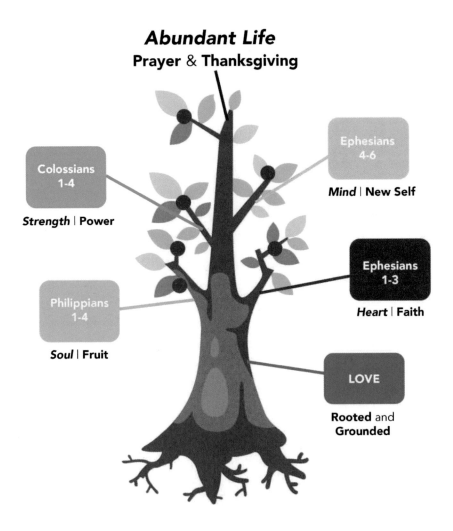

Abundant Life
Prayer & Thanksgiving

Ephesians 4-6
Mind | **New Self**

Colossians 1-4
Strength | **Power**

Ephesians 1-3
Heart | **Faith**

Philippians 1-4
Soul | **Fruit**

LOVE
Rooted and **Grounded**

ABIDE IN JESUS: THE TRUE VINE

At the beginning of each Bible study week, I use Paul's teachings and journey into taking root or hold of the abundant life to tell my own story. I realize that I cannot ask you to share your story with others if I am not willing to disclose my own. But first, let us pray.

Heavenly Father,

I ask that You prune off the enemy's strongholds on our life as we stand **rooted and grounded in love** and built up in the fullness of Christ. I pray that You will weed out our habitual sins (thorns) with a desire to pursue the **heart** of Jesus and follow His example as we grow in our **faith**.

I pray that You will till the soil of our **minds** to focus on the things above and transform us to reflect the **new self** in Christ. Lord, I ask that You sow within us the seeds of truth as You enable us to persevere in the **power** of Your **strength**. As we stand firm in the hope of the glory of God, our **souls** become filled with the **fruit of righteousness** that comes through your Son, Jesus.

For we know the harvest belongs to You, Lord. And, in due season, we will reap a harvest of blessings, if we commit our lives to You and do not give up. We give You all the glory, honor, and praise as the Holy Spirit shows us how to seek You first, abide in the True Vine, serve others in love, and bear fruit for your Kingdom. In Jesus's name, I pray. Amen.

Be rooted and built up in Christ, and established in the Faith, as you have been taught, abounding in it with thanksgiving.

Colossians 2:7 (ESV)

TABLE OF CONTENTS

Section I

Section II

Appendix – Reader's Guide

FOREWORD

Bridget's goal for writing this book is to demonstrate that the Bible is still relevant, exciting, and comprehensive even in today's culture. Bridget walks you through Paul's prison letters to explain the foundational principles of Christianity and Jesus's command to spread the good news of the gospel to all the nations.

Through this Bible study, Bridget inspires the reader to adopt St. Paul's mission and purpose, which is to be an individual who desires to see the Gospel of Jesus Christ brought to the world. Through her testimony and Bible lessons, Bridget reminds us that there is no substitute for the evidence of a changed life.

Therefore, teaching others around us is of no use if we deny our faith by our lifestyle. This book applies to new and seasoned believers who may need a reminder of how to walk according to God's calling and purpose, "so that you may live a life worthy of the Lord and please him in every way: bearing fruit in every good work, growing in the knowledge of God."— Colossians 1:10

Dr. Blanche Hunt

SECTION I

For **God** so loved the world that he *gave his one and only Son,* that whoever believes in him shall not perish but have *eternal life.*

John 3:16 (NIV)

1

THE LAW OF CHRIST

Jesus said, "Do not think that I have come to abolish the Law or the Prophets; I have not come to abolish them but to fulfill them" (Matthew 5:17).

The Ten Commandments in the Old Testament are summed up by God's greatest commandment: *Love.* For the commandments, "You shall not commit adultery, You shall not murder, You shall not steal, You shall not covet," and any other commandment, are summed up in this word: "You shall love your neighbor as yourself." Love does no wrong to a neighbor; therefore, *love* is the fulfilling of the law" (Romans 13:8 – 10, ESV).

"For what the (Old Testament) law was powerless to do because it was weakened by the (sinful) flesh, God did by sending his own Son in the <u>likeness</u> of sinful flesh to be a sin offering. And so, He condemned sin in the flesh (Christ), in order that the righteous requirement of the law (love) might be fully met in us, who do not live according to the flesh but according to the Spirit" (Romans 8:3 – 4).

Therefore, "If you confess with your mouth that Jesus is Lord and believe in your heart that God raised Him from the dead, you will be saved. For with the heart one believes and is **justified**, and with the mouth one confesses and is saved" (Romans 10:9-10, ESV).

Believers in Jesus are **transformed** and promised eternal life through the gift of the Holy Spirit. Therefore, be a reflection of Christ to sinners in a lost world and bear fruit by the Spirit (**application**).

Paul encouraged believers to seek the hope of God's glory and grace by obeying God's Word and walking in the Spirit daily so they may experience **sanctification** and have an intimate and personal relationship with the Father through His Son. As a result, Jesus, the Savior of the world, gets all of the glory for our justification, transformation, application, and sanctification.

I am the *vine*; you are the *branches*. If you remain in me, and I in you, you will *bear much fruit.*

John 15:1-3

CHAPTER

2

FROM LOST TO FOUND

It was 2014 and my husband, Jim, and I decided to get a Doberman puppy for Christmas. We named him Max. I never had a dog that I could call my very own. Jim grew up with pets and had several dogs in adulthood. I had no idea what to expect from nurturing this adorable creature. My first responsibility every morning was to walk Max outside in our yard, which gave me the opportunity to engage in my favorite pastime activity, pondering.

I usually ponder while sitting on the couch reading or listening to music, but walking Max gave me the chance to think outside. I didn't realize it at the time, but it allowed me to spend time exploring God's beauty. I observed how green the trees were again, how the sun felt on my face, and the breeze in my hair. Jim has two large berry gardens with an assortment of fruit plants in our backyard. I even began to notice when the fruit would grow and prosper on the vines.

One day, Jim wanted to cut down all the shrubs that formed a perfect line around our front porch and replace it with a variety of grape plants. I thought no one in this neighborhood or anywhere has a vineyard in their front yard. He said it needed direct sunlight and the front yard would be the perfect spot. I began to reason with the idea.

We do have several huge trees in our backyard, and it is extremely shaded. Plus, he planted the berry gardens in the only place in our yard that had semi-direct sunlight. After much thought, I agreed. I didn't know what to expect. Yes, people in town noticed and asked how our grapes were doing. I would say, "They're doing just fine and growing like a weed. How are your kids doing?" I'd quickly change the subject to avoid further questioning.

What I didn't expect as I walked Max every morning was how much I would learn from watching the vines, branches, and the grapes grow. I had never studied botany, but God was showing and teaching me about the one True Vine. I remember taking pictures of the new grapes on my phone and showing my friend Blanche at work what I had observed.

I told her, "See, this is the primary food source, the strong vine, and all these branches grow and extend from the vine, then all of the branches begin to grow leaves, and eventually, the branches produce fruit." I sounded like an excited kindergartner learning something new for the first time who had to share her discovery with a friend.

The parable of the vine and the branches was the exact spark of inspiration that I needed. Instead of feeling like walking Max was an everyday chore, I began to see it as time spent in the pasture, like David. I started asking God questions, "What do you want to show or teach me today, Lord?" I would wait in anticipation for an answer.

I felt in touch with God again and surrounded by His beauty. When I took the time to look around my backyard, I began to rediscover God's presence and peace again. I was learning to commune with Him. Then, I thought about Adam and Eve. How God created them for that very purpose, to collaborate and build a relationship with their Creator.

So, that was my mission while walking Max in the pasture. I began to seek answers from God. One day I asked Him, "Is this it, Lord? Is this all there is? There has to be more to life than this. There has to be more to living than having a big house, a new car, a dream job, or vacation." Deep down, I knew that there was. I said, "God, show me what you want me to do with my life?"

The answer wasn't immediate. He gently whispered to my heart that morning, "Continue to seek me first. Then I will show you what to do." Of course, I wasn't perfect. I would walk the line for a short time and then fall back into old sinful habits. Then, I would remember my conversation with God and try again. I noticed this had been the cycle my entire Christian life. Walk the line, fall, stay down for a while (sometimes years), eventually get back up again, temporarily walk the line, and press repeat.

Once again, I asked God "Isn't there more to life than this habitual cycle of set free, sin, repent, forgiveness, set free, sin, repent, forgiveness?" He said, "Yes, my child, but you never listened to my first instruction." God said again, "Seek me first." So, I went back into the pasture to listen and learn.

Yes, I was stubborn. I would fall back into the sin cycle and hit repeat time and time again. I kept asking God, "What is my problem?" I felt like Paul when he said, "Why do I continue to do the very things that I hate? Why can't I get this Christian thing right? Why is it so hard to follow the rules?" God gently said to me, "Bridget, it's not about following the rules, it's about having a relationship with me. All I ask is that you seek me first, have faith, and abide in me." I thought, but *how?*

My mind recalled a story in Matthew when Jesus was in a boat with His disciples. They were so fearful of drowning in a storm. Jesus replied to them, *"Oh you of little faith, why are you so afraid?"* I felt like Jesus was saying to me, "Oh Bridget of little faith, you don't believe that I can do all the things that I've been teaching you in the pasture." I thought, what do you mean, Jesus? Are you saying that *I* have a lack of faith? I believe that you died on the cross for my sins. I accepted you into my heart as Lord and Savior when I was twelve. I did this. I did that. I even tried to follow the rules of good Christian living.

But, Jesus interrupted my thoughts and spoke to my heart, "Yes, you are saved and have been justified by faith. It's not about what you've done. It's about what I've already done for you. Are you ready to take the next step of faith and ask me to transform you into the person that I created you to be?" I gasped and surrendered with, "Yes, Lord." He said, "What is the second part of the verse?" I responded, *"But seek ye first the kingdom of God, **and His righteousness**, and all* *these things shall be added unto you" (Matthew 6:33, KJV).*

Around this time of enlightenment, I saw on social media that my former doctoral classmate, Brenda Randle, was having a women's conference on the college campus where I worked. Out of curiosity and a desire to catch up with Brenda, I registered for the conference in the spring of 2016. I asked my friend Blanche to join me. She accepted. I didn't know what to expect, but the conference theme was *"How to Birth Your Vision."* If that doesn't pique your interest, I don't know what will.

During my doctoral program, I sat next to Brenda every Tuesday night for two years. I knew that Brenda was a woman of God. I admired the fact that she did not hide her faith the way that I did. I hadn't spoken to Brenda since we completed our coursework. I had no idea what God was doing in her life until I attended the conference.

Brenda's conference on birthing your vision refreshed and rejuvenated me. I told God that I would take a leap of faith and sign up with Brenda to coach and mentor me in writing a book. Before I left the conference, I committed to working with Brenda. I knew if I had left without signing an agreement that I would talk myself out of it.

Brenda explained that I could sign-up for an online group or enroll in an individual training program. I agreed to the individual training. I told her that I needed to get through the end of the spring semester before I could meet with her. Brenda and I made arrangements to have our first session in June. We had a game plan for the book. I would use the summer months to start writing. I went full speed into research and writing mode for the entire month.

I distinctly remember it was a Thursday morning in early July. I was getting ready to take Max outside when I received a text that stated we had lost our dear friend, Suzanne. I stood frozen with immediate tears flowing from my eyes. How can this be? She was in remission. She had beat breast cancer after battling for two years. Yes, she was tired all of the time. She rarely felt good, but the cancer was gone. But, something went wrong.

She was rushed to the hospital the day before and passed away the next day. Suzanne was my closest friend. I was hurt, devastated, and confused by the sudden loss. I began spending more time in the pasture looking for answers. I was extremely down and out. I didn't feel like writing or doing anything for the next three months.

I remember walking Max one day in October. I just broke down and said, "What is this all about, Lord? Why did you take my best friend from me? Why did she have to die so young? Why? Why? Why?" With tears streaming down my face, I looked up into the heavens. I felt the sunlight on my face and a cool breeze flow through my hair. I noticed the leaves on the trees shaking as if they were clapping while the wind blew swiftly through the air.

God said, "You didn't lose anything. Suzanne is always with you, in your heart, and so am I. You can hear her laughter in the breeze and see her smile in the clouds. She is so happy and free. Rejoice with her and look forward to seeing her again someday." I said, "Yes, Lord, but I dearly miss our earthly friendship, lunch dates, and girl outings, but I know that she is always with me. I know that she is praying for me, cheering me on, and encouraging me to press on and fight the good fight of faith."

I imagine her saying to me, "Oh, Bridget, if I had only known then what I know now, I would be sharing my faith in Jesus with everyone I know and meet." I can hear her say, "Don't wait until heaven. Get to know and experience the hope and the glory of the Lord here on earth. You can know His fullness; experience His abundance and power in your life, right now!"

I called Brenda the next week and told her that I was ready to write again. I told her that I wanted to change directions and write about *how the habitual sins of the old self prevent Christians from seeking God first and living in His righteousness.* As I began to research the topic, I came across a theory that said Paul's thorn in the flesh (habitual sin) might have been a temptation or a health problem. I knew the basic story about Paul's conversion on the Road to Damascus, but that was about it.

As I studied the book of Acts, I got to know Paul. He felt like someone that I could relate to and carry on a conversation with over lunch. Paul's struggles, missionary journeys, letters, and imprisonment not only increased his abiding faith in God, but he also developed a personal relationship with Him. This type of commitment became my spiritual goal, as well.

The Apostle Paul wrote 13 letters or books of the New Testament. He addressed most of his letters to the early churches. The other apostles and congregates accepted Paul's letters and teachings as God's inspired word given to him through the power of the Holy Spirit.

As I read Paul's letters, it became apparent to me that he understood how to have a relationship with Jesus and live the abundant life. Paul held the secret to the mystery that I was looking for my entire life. I became determined to figure it out for myself and learn from his experiences. Hence, the reason I tell Paul's thorn story along with my own.

His thorn, my thorn, your thorn, it's all the same. No matter the thorn. The question remains, which thorn is keeping you in the habitual sin cycle and from having a personal, intimate relationship with Jesus? You can discover the answer to this question and so much more through Paul's letters and the workbook, *Rooted: Growing in Christ*.

If you know in your heart there is more to life than *this*, I would like to invite you to join me on an exciting journey of self-discovery. I pray that you will. God Bless you for taking a step of faith and trusting the Holy Spirit to show you how to grow, abide, and live in the fullness and abundance of the true vine, Jesus Christ.

3

FROM SAUL TO PAUL

For generations, Israelites (Jews) had lived by the old covenant God made with Moses. Righteousness (to be set apart for God) was based on the Law of Moses (Ten Commandments). However, Israel extended the Law of Moses to include 613 moral, civic, and religious laws for the Jews to follow.

For what the Law could not do (save us) because it was weakened by the flesh or sinful nature, God did by sending His Only Son. *"But when the set time had fully come, God sent his Son, born of a woman, born under the law, to redeem those under the law, that we might receive adoption to sonship" (Galatians 4:4 –5). (Refer to God's Covenants in the Appendix, page 115)*

After Jesus's crucifixion and resurrection, those who had faith in Jesus met resistance from the legalistic Jews, who were strictly faithful to the Law. They did not want to give up their beliefs, customs, and laws to believe that Jesus is the Messiah (Savior). They did not want to accept that there was now no condemnation under the Law for those who are in Jesus. *"For the **law of the Spirit** of life has set you free in Christ Jesus from the Law of sin and death" (Romans 8:2, ESV).*

On the Day of Pentecost, when believers in Jesus received the ***Holy Spirit*** in Jerusalem, they began to share with others that Jesus is the path to freedom and righteousness, instead of law-keeping. One of these believers was a Deacon named Stephen. He was filled with wisdom and the power of the Holy Spirit. He did great wonders and signs among the people (Acts 6:8).

While Stephen was teaching about the Son of God in the Jerusalem Synagogue, the Jews became angry and began to argue with him. They could not endure the words of the Holy Spirit that were coming from Stephen. Some members of the audience began to conspire and secretly frame Stephen by accusing him of speaking blasphemous words against Moses and God.

They dragged Stephen before the Sanhedrin Council. The Council cast him out of the city. The witnesses laid their garments at the feet of a man named **Saul** as they stoned Stephen to death. Stephen was the first martyr for the sake of Christ. *(Refer to The Christian Movement in the Appendix page 117)*

Saul of Tarsus was a Jewish man (Pharisee) highly educated in Judaism law, a Roman citizen, and a member of the Sanhedrin Council. Saul loved and upheld the Law of Moses, but hated and persecuted the followers of Jesus. After the stoning of Stephen, *"Saul was still breathing out murderous threats against the Lord's disciples. He went to the high priest"* (Acts 9:1). He asked the high priest to send letters to the Synagogue in Damascus requesting permission for him to travel there and arrest any believers of Jesus and bring them back to Jerusalem as prisoners.

The high priest granted permission to Saul. Two men traveled with Saul on the road to Damascus. "Now as he (Saul) went on his way, he approached Damascus, and suddenly a light from heaven shone around him. And falling to the ground, he heard a voice saying to him, *"Saul, Saul, why are you persecuting me?"* And he said, *"Who are you, Lord?"* And he said, *"I am Jesus, whom you are persecuting. But rise and enter the city, and you will be told what you are to do."* The men who were traveling with him stood speechless, hearing the voice but seeing no one" (Acts 9:3 – 7, ESV).

Saul went to Damascus as a blind man and did not eat or drink for three days. God told Ananias, a disciple at Damascus, in a vision to visit and lay his hands upon Saul. At first, Ananias questioned God because he had heard about murderous Saul and how much he hated believers. But the Lord said to him, *"Go, for he is a chosen instrument of mine to carry my name before the Gentiles and kings and the children of Israel. For I will show him how much he must suffer for the sake of my name"* (Acts 9:15 – 16, ESV).

Ananias went to the house where Saul was and told him that the Lord had sent him. As Ananias laid his hands upon Saul, the scales fell from his eyes, he regained his sight, and became filled with the Holy Spirit. Saul rose and was baptized.

Let us ponder this life-changing event for a moment. Mean, evil, arrogant Saul, whom not only Christians feared, but most Jews because of his high standing on the Sanhedrin Council and for receiving the best Judaism education there ever was, just surrendered all to Jesus.

Right now, I want you to identify someone that you think will never surrender his/her life to Jesus. They may be mean, hateful, unrepentant, or just refuse to believe. Let me say this, if the voice of God can make malicious Saul fall to the ground on his knees and confess, He has your person in the palm of His hand. Keep praying for him or her. If Jesus saved Saul, he will do the same for your friend or loved one.

Afterward, Saul spent several days with the supporters of Jesus in Damascus. "At once he began to preach in the synagogues that Jesus is the Son of God. All those who heard him were astonished and asked, *"Isn't he the man who raised havoc in Jerusalem among those who call on this name? And hasn't he come here to take them as prisoners to the chief priests?"* Yet Saul grew more and more powerful and baffled the Jews living in Damascus by proving that Jesus is the Messiah.

After many days had gone by, there was a conspiracy among the Jews to kill him, but Saul learned of their plan. Day and night, they kept close watch on the city gates in order to kill him. But his followers took him by night and lowered him in a basket through an opening in the wall" (Acts 9:20 – 25).

"When he (Saul) came to Jerusalem, he tried to join the Apostles, but they were all afraid of him, not believing that he really was a disciple. But Barnabas took him and brought him to the Apostles.

He told them how Saul on his journey had seen the Lord and that the Lord had spoken to him, and how in Damascus he had preached fearlessly in the name of Jesus. So, Saul stayed with them and moved about freely in Jerusalem, speaking boldly in the name of the Lord.

He talked and debated with the Hellenistic (Greek-speaking) Jews, but they tried to kill him. When the believers learned of this, they took him down to Caesarea and sent him off to Tarsus. Then the church throughout Judea, Galilee and Samaria enjoyed a time of peace and was strengthened. Living in the fear of the Lord and encouraged by the Holy Spirit, it (the church) increased in numbers" (Acts 9:26 – 31).

Saul returned to his hometown in Tarsus for his protection. During this time of refuge, Saul preached in the surrounding region and prepared for the works of service that God had planned for him to do. Saul went by his Hebrew name until he was commissioned by God to spread the gospel of grace to the Gentiles. Afterwards, he went by his Roman name, Paul.[1] *"However, I consider my life worth nothing to me; my only aim is to finish the race and complete the task the Lord Jesus has given me—the task of testifying to the good news of* **God's grace***"* (Acts 20:24).

Paul was hand-picked to reveal the mystery of God (the New Covenant) to the Gentiles, which was kept hidden from all the prophets in the Old Testament, until now. "The apostle Paul often spoke of such "mysteries": Jesus' incarnation (1 Timothy 3:16), the indwelling of the Spirit (Colossians 1:26–27), the unity of the church (Ephesians 3:4–6), the rapture (1 Corinthians 15:51–52), and the gospel itself (Colossians 4:3). All these truths were "hidden" from the prophets of old but have been revealed plainly to us today. They are "mysteries" that are no longer mysterious to the child of God. "The mystery of faith" is the divinely revealed truth about grace, redemption, and forgiveness in Christ."[2]

4

FROM JERUSALEM TO ROME

Before Paul's imprisonment in Rome, God's plan for him included three missionary journeys to help establish and build up the body of Christ. During his travels, he taught and ministered to the nations and wrote letters to the surrounding churches to share the gospel of grace with others. Paul taught how salvation and reconciliation to God through His Resurrected Son, Jesus Christ, are promised to ALL people, both the Jews and Gentiles.

During Paul's **first** (45 – 47 A.D.) and **second** journey (51 – 53 A.D.), he preached, taught, and founded churches throughout Asia Minor (Turkey) and Europe. During Paul's **third** missionary journey (54 – 58 A.D.), he revisited the existing churches that he founded. The purpose of this trip was to encourage the churches and seek donations to help feed the poor Christians living in Jerusalem. At this time, Jerusalem had chronic poverty and food shortages. It was overly crowded and heavily taxed by the Romans. This effort was known as the Jerusalem Collection.

Paul's teachings on the gospel of grace and faith in the death and resurrection of Jesus Christ for the forgiveness of sins had spread, influenced, and converted thousands upon thousands of people to Christianity. Asking Israel, who obeyed the old covenant since the days of Moses, to exchange their established traditions and beliefs for a new covenant did not sit well with them.

Therefore, Paul had enemies throughout all the nations for teaching that salvation is a gift of God's grace and only attainable through faith in Jesus Christ. Think of it this way, Paul was on the world's top 10 most wanted list, and some people wanted him captured – dead or alive. *(Refer to The Missionary Journeys of Paul in the appendix, page 125)*

At the end of Paul's third missionary journey, he arrived in Jerusalem. Soon after, Paul was falsely accused for desecrating the temple by bringing a Gentile with him. He was brought before the chief priests, the Sanhedrin, and eventually Governor Festus. Paul appealed the charges against him to Caesar and was sent to Rome.

There were 276 passengers, including Paul, aboard the ship to Rome. Midway through the trip, a storm pushed the ship to Malta where it was shipwrecked. While the soldiers repaired the ship for three months, Paul preached and performed miracles among the people. They boarded the ship again and eventually landed in Rome where Paul was imprisoned for two years.

Map: Paul's Missionary Journeys. https://www.conformingtojesus.com/images/webpages/pauls_journeys_map1.jpg

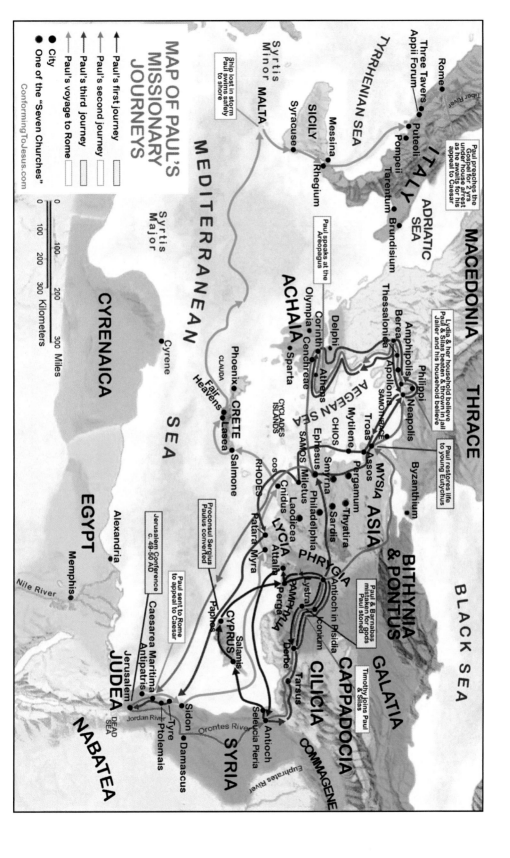

MAP OF PAUL'S MISSIONARY JOURNEYS

ConformingToJesus.com

Legend:
- → Paul's first journey
- → Paul's second journey
- → Paul's third journey
- → Paul's voyage to Rome
- ● City
- ● One of the "Seven Churches"

Scale:
0 100 200 300 Kilometers
0 100 200 300 Miles

Annotation boxes:

- Paul preaches the undisputable Gospel for 2 yrs as he awaits for his arrest appeal to Caesar
- Ship lost in storm Paul swims safely to shore
- Paul speaks at the Areopagus
- Lydia & her household believe. Paul & Silas beaten & thrown in jail. Jailer and his household believe
- Paul restores life to young Eutychus
- Paul & Barnabas mistaken for gods Paul stoned
- Timothy joins Paul & Silas
- Proconsul Sergius Paulus converted
- Jerusalem Conference c. 49-50 AD
- Paul sent to Rome to appeal to Caesar

Regions: MACEDONIA, THRACE, BLACK SEA, TYRRHENIAN SEA, ADRIATIC SEA, ITALY, SICILY, MALTA, MEDITERRANEAN SEA, ACHAIA, AEGEAN SEA, MYSIA, ASIA, BITHYNIA & PONTUS, GALATIA, CAPPADOCIA, PHRYGIA, LYCIA, PAMPHYLIA, CILICIA, COMMAGENE, SYRIA, JUDEA, NABATEA, EGYPT, CYRENAICA, CRETE, RHODES, CYPRUS, CYCLADES ISLANDS

Cities/places: Rome, Three Taverns, Appii Forum, Puteoli, Pompeii, Messina, Rhegium, Tarentum, Brundisium, Syracuse, Byzantium, Philippi, Neapolis, Amphipolis, Apollonia, Thessalonica, Berea, SAMOTHRACE, Troas, Assos, Olympia, Corinth, Cenchreae, Delphi, Athens, Sparta, Mytilene, CHIOS, Ephesus, Smyrna, Pergamum, SAMOS, Miletus, Thyatira, Sardis, Philadelphia, Laodicea, Cnidus, COS, Patara, Myra, Attalia, Perga, Antioch in Pisidia, Iconium, Lystra, Derbe, Paphos, Salamis, Tarsus, Antioch, Seleucia Pieria, Sidon, Damascus, Tyre, Ptolemais, Caesarea Maritima, Antipatris, Jerusalem, Phoenix, Fair Heavens, Lasea, Salmone, CLAUDA, Cyrene, Alexandria, Memphis

Seas/waters: Syrtis Minor, Syrtis Major, Tiber River, Nile River, Orontes River, Euphrates River, Jordan River, DEAD SEA

CHAPTER

5

THE PRISON LETTERS
61-63 A.D.

While Paul was under house arrest for two years in Rome awaiting his trial before Caesar, he wrote letters to the church leaders in Ephesus, Colossae, Philippi, and to his friend Philemon. Paul had planted several churches during the three missionary journeys. He wanted to ensure that the church leaders were walking in a manner that was worthy of the gospel, standing firm, and striving together in one Spirit for the faith. The leaders shared Paul's letters with the house churches throughout the surrounding regions. These writings are known as The Prison Letters.

Ephesians

Ephesus was a Roman capital and the epicenter of Paul's ministry. It was one of the four largest cities in the Roman Empire with over 250,000 people. While imprisoned, Paul wrote to the church at Ephesus to remind them of their spiritual blessings in Christ. Paul revealed God's mystery or will for salvation. *"But because of his great love for us, God, who is rich in mercy, made us alive with Christ even when we were dead in transgressions—it is by grace you have been saved" (Eph. 2:4 – 5) "through faith—and this is not from yourselves, it is the gift of God" (Eph. 2:8).* Paul explained how the new covenant replaced the old one to unite the Jews and

Gentiles into one Church, one body of Christ. Paul also gave the Ephesians' instructions for Christian living by taking off the old self and its deceitful desires and putting on the new self, created to be like God in true righteousness and holiness.

Colossians

Out of concern, Paul wrote to the Colossians to help strengthen their hope and faith in the true teachings of the gospel. He encouraged them to *"set your minds on the things above, and not on earthly things" (Col.3:2)* and protect your thoughts from the false prophets and teachings that were spreading in the land. Paul's letter to the Colossians is a reminder of the love, compassion, and prayer concerns we should have for other believers' temptations and struggles. He wrote this letter in a spirit of gratitude while praying for them to receive knowledge on how to live, apply, and abide in God's perfect and pleasing will.

Philippians

Paul encouraged the Philippians to count their persecutions and sufferings for Christ's sake as an eternal gain. They were concerned about their acts of righteousness and ability to spread the gospel while they too were being persecuted. Paul asked them to *"make my joy complete by being like-minded, having the same love, being one in spirit and of one mind" (Phil. 2:2)* as they shared the gospel of grace with others. He asked them to humbly and persistently have faith in the promises of God, to bear witness, and to serve others out of love by having the utmost respect for God. Then, they could experience the fullness of *His* overflowing joy. He prayed the Philippians would understand how their unity, joyfulness, and obedience in Christ magnified and glorified the Lord.

Map: First Century Aegean Region. Reprinted with permission from Lucidity Information Design, LLC. http://www.lucidityid.com

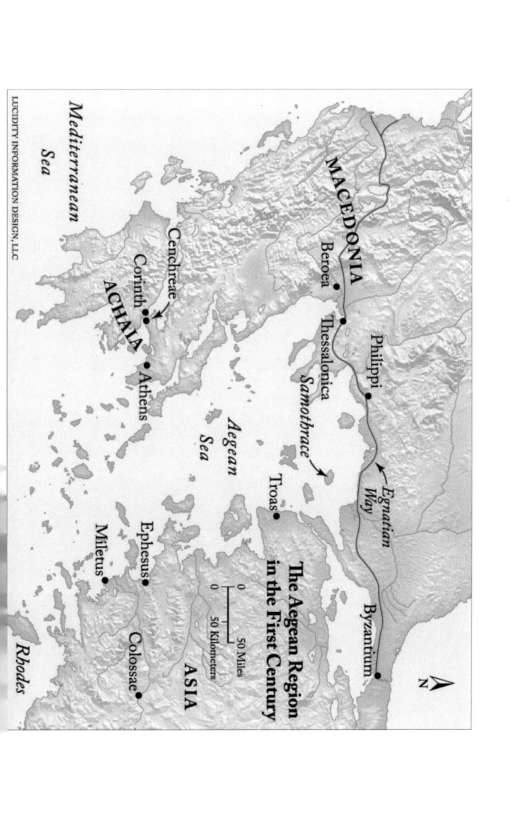

The Aegean Region in the First Century

MACEDONIA

Beroea

Thessalonica

Samothrace

Philippi

Egnatian Way

Byzantium

Troas

Cenchreae

Corinth

ACHAIA

Athens

Aegean Sea

Ephesus

Miletus

Colossae

ASIA

Rhodes

Mediterranean Sea

0 — 50 Miles
0 — 50 Kilometers

N

SECTION II

For all have *sinned* and fall short of the *glory of God.*

Romans 3:23 (NIV)

Week 1

HABITUAL SINS

"I would not have known what sin was had it not been for the law. For I would not have known what coveting really was if the law had not said, 'You shall not covet.'" (Romans 7:7)

Paul's Thorn

The purpose of the Law was for the Jews to become aware of their sins. Paul preached that no law would ever be able to save or make us righteous. He said if righteousness could be achieved through adherence to the Law or by good works then Jesus died for nothing. Everyone is a sinner and righteousness can only be found through faith in Jesus Christ alone, not the Law.

Therefore, Paul learned that obeying or "dying" to the Law did not prevent him from doing what he hated most, his indwelling or habitual sins. These are the same sins that he kept committing and giving to God over and over again and asking for the same forgiveness. Can you relate?

Paul had a thorn in the flesh, a messenger of Satan, to torment him. Some Bible scholars say this thorn was a speech impediment, physical disability, temptation, or an actual person who followed him around during his ministry to undermine or discredit him. Paul never shared his thorn with us, but we all have our thorns that we keep hidden from others, and like Adam and Eve, we even try to hide them from God.

In the book of Romans, Paul could not resist and overcome temptations in his own strength; instead, he allowed his feelings (heart), thoughts (mind), and flesh (will) to control his behavior (soul). He could not reconcile in his mind what his old self desired versus the new self. They were in constant opposition, waging war.

Paul said, *"I do not understand myself. I want to do what is right, but I do not do it. Instead, I do the very thing I hate" (Romans 7:15, NLV).* Paul asked God three times to take this thorn of torment from him, but God's answer was always a resounding, No. God told Paul, *"My grace is sufficient for you, for my power is made perfect in (your) weakness" (2 Corinthians 12:9).*

He knew that he was no longer a slave to sin and under the performance of religious rules but under God's grace. He realized by having a grateful attitude of humility, thoughts of forgiveness, and surrendering his will (strength) to God, Jesus could work through him to help him overcome his habitual sins. Paul said, *"Therefore I will boast all the more gladly about my weaknesses, so that Christ's power may rest on me" (2 Corinthians 12:9).*

Paul's weaknesses kept him from being prideful, arrogant, or conceited in his ministry. He was able to rejoice in the hope of the glory of God and make sure that Jesus received all of the praise, rather than himself. Paul said, *"That is why, for Christ's sake, I delight in weaknesses, in insults, in hardships, in persecutions, in difficulties. For when I am weak, then I am strong" (2 Corinthians 12:10).*

My Thorn

Your story, Paul's, and my own are no surprise to God. He knew how our stories would unfold and end before he created us in our mother's womb. He sent the first seed of righteousness, Jesus, born of a virgin to take away our hurt, all the sins of the world, and reconcile us to a Holy God. If you belong to Christ, then you are the spiritual seed of Abraham and heirs according to God's covenant promise.

Anyone who is in Christ is a new creation. The old life has gone; a new life has begun.

Throughout this Bible study, I will share with you the broken branches of my old life. What I did not know how to do at the age of 13, I am doing now at the age of 43. After thirty years of searching, I am taking a stand and focusing on the things above and seeking God's approval, rather than the approval of others.

By completing the workbook activities, you too can discover your brokenness, the pathway to healing, and the steps to abundant living. So, as I take a deep breath, here goes the first part of my story.

My older brother had a friend; I will call him "Pete," that was always kind to me and showed me a lot of attention when I was around the age of four. I looked up to my brother's friend and soon developed a crush on him.

One day we were alone in my brother's bedroom talking and lying on the bottom bunk bed with the door shut. Pete began to caress my face and hair. I felt loved and comforted by him. I trusted him. He kissed my cheek, my lips, and then stuck his tongue in my mouth. I had seen couples passionately kiss on soap operas before so I knew what was happening. His affection made me feel special.

Suddenly, we heard my brother burst into the house talking and laughing with some other friends. Pete jumped up from the bed and started playing a video game. My brother opened the door to his room and said, "Come on we're starting a ball game." I don't even think my brother noticed me lying frozen on the bed. They both left the room. I laid there deep in my little girl thoughts.

After this encounter, I began to fantasize about Pete. I thought about those movie stars and women on TV. How beautiful, glamorous, and desirable they were to those men who flattered and flirted with them. I wanted to look like, act like, and be like them with Pete. I became obsessed with Pete. I began to wonder where he was, when he would come over next, and when I could receive his attention again.

One rainy afternoon, my mom, my brother, his friends, and I were watching a TV show in the living room. Craving Pete's attention, I

Every *weakness* you have is an *opportunity* for God to show His *strength* in your life.

Adapted from 2 Corinthians 12:9

bravely crawled into his chair to sit on his lap. I guess no one thought it was strange or even noticed since I was always around and following my brother and his friends.

I had on shorts or a dress and my favorite blanket in hand. I distinctly remember wanting to feel that warmth and comfort from him again. I curled up to him with my blanket. He made his move. His hands were not in sight, so he slipped his finger underneath my panties and began to rub the inside of that area. I did not understand what had just happened, but I did know that it felt different and I felt loved and wanted.

A loss of innocence opens your eyes to the things of the world that were meant to be revealed to you much later in life. Even though my mind could not comprehend it, I became aware of the feelings of intimacy. This experience fueled my obsession with my brother's friend. I followed him around the house, outside, anywhere I could get close to him.

My brother told me to get lost one day while he and his friends were playing video games in his room. I asked him where Pete was and he said, "He's with his girlfriend." Then, he pushed me out of his room and closed the door. I was so upset. A girlfriend? What about me? I thought I was his girlfriend. I went to my room, laid on my bed, and cried myself to sleep. I was sad and hurt by this news.

At this point, you may be wondering, why is she sharing this about herself? Because the thorns of passivity and unforgiveness were the core reasons why I could not practice or live out my freedom in Christ. The molestation planted the seed. This incident, among other things, took root and hold of the hurt, distrust, and the feelings of unworthiness that I experienced most of my life.

As the roots began to develop into stems, thorns of pride and rebellion grew into seasons of withdrawal, self-consciousness, and disobedience. Over the years, the thorn of pride pierced my heart; rebellion controlled my mind and alcohol fueled my flesh. I concealed and found relief from the pain of my past by engaging in these habits to sustain and fulfill me.

I kept the molestation hidden within me until around the age of ten. One day, I told my brother what his friend had done, but he didn't believe me. He asked Pete about it the next day at school, and he called me a liar. After that, I dropped the issue and never mentioned it to anyone again.

When I was twelve, my grandfather became ill and bed-ridden. I was feeling confused about religion and had all these questions on how to be saved. I went into my grandfather's room alone to speak with him about my confusion. He just laid there and listened. I didn't know if he understood what I was saying, but I was crying and needed a sounding board.

After a while, my dad entered the room to spend time with his father. Dad did not seem to notice me. He began talking and carrying on a conversation with my grandfather. In the middle of my dad's sentence, my grandfather said, "Quiet son, let Bridget talk." My dad looked at me as if to say, "*talk about what?*" With tear-filled eyes, I told my dad that I wanted to know how to be saved. My grandfather motioned for him to lead me in the prayer of salvation. So, he did.

I remember going to school feeling reserved and socially awkward as I was trying to understand the change that I had experienced by accepting Christ as my Savior. I did not dare tell my friends about my salvation. I never talked about Jesus with my friends. I did not know if they were Christians or not. I experienced this incredible joy but did not know how to share it with others or live like a Christian.

My mother was a Catholic and my father, a Protestant. My father converted to Catholicism in the 60s to marry my mom. My family and I attended the Catholic Church until I was twelve years old. Soon after I became saved, my dad decided he wanted our family to leave the Catholic Church and join the Baptist Church. I was familiar with the Protestant faith and teachings because my brother and I attended church, listened to taped sermons, had bible studies, and sang gospel songs with my dad's parents as far back as I can remember.

I believe the change in church membership prompted my desire and curiosity of wanting to know how to live a Christian life. Shortly after that, my immediate family converted, and we were all baptized in the Baptist church. I attended Wednesday night, Sunday morning and evening services every week. I even went to church camp, but I never learned how to have an intimate, personal relationship with my Savior and Creator. I had to wing it.

I did not know how to pray and just thought I was supposed to feel guilty and ashamed of my sins all of the time. Eventually, when I got into trouble or sinned, these feelings would lead me to repent, ask for forgiveness, and try to "live" right until the next time I messed up and felt incredible guilt or regret for my sins. At the time, I wasn't aware that this pattern of behavior had a name. It is called the habitual sin cycle.

Growing up around my paternal grandparents, they emphasized two main teachings or Godly principles to my brother and me; #1. Your body is a temple of God; do not abuse it with drugs or alcohol and #2. Always strive to be virtuous by abstaining from sex. These two principals were a huge deal to my grandmother and her two daughters. For whatever reason, I believed these were the unpardonable sins. I grew up in fear of drinking alcohol or abusing drugs and most certainly swore to them that I would never have sex until I was married.

By ninth-grade, my friends began experimenting with alcohol and boys. Based on my guilt and fear, there was no way I was going to engage in such behaviors. When my friends figured out that I was not going to participate with them, they dropped me hotter than a two-dollar pistol. They did not invite me to parties anymore, sleepovers, or hang out with me outside of school. It didn't help matters much that I was going through puberty, depressed, and not very outgoing during this period in my life.

They were still my friends and kind to me at school, but they didn't want me to tattle or make them feel like I was judging them. I felt like such a loner for standing up for my beliefs. I did not talk to my parents about it or anyone else. For most of that year, I felt left out and spent most of my free time with my family or cousins. I did not have the wisdom or know how to create a new circle of friends who had the same values or beliefs as me.

The Wednesday night Bible study that I attended as a young teenager was for having fun, eating, talking about a Bible story or lesson, but it did not teach you how to apply the biblical principles or lessons to your everyday life. The church did not offer a class on how to be a new Christian, how to resist the temptations of sin, or how to develop a relationship with Jesus.

Therefore, I wrote this Bible study as a Christian orientation for new and returning believers of the faith. No one had told me that there are steps to living the Christian life. Christianity does not end after going through the plan of salvation. This is only the beginning. The Christian life is an exciting progression of understanding and working out your salvation to become more like the image of Christ.

After my redemption, life went back to normal. I did not understand or know how to make the transition from unbeliever to Christianity. My friends remained the same, and so did my habits. Based on my feelings of loneliness and a desire to be liked or win the approval of my friends, I decided to live my life as an unbeliever.

I was an impressionable teenager and easily persuaded by my older peers. One summer night a much older friend picked me up at my house. She had a six-pack of beer in the car. She told me to go ahead and try one. I was 15 and had never drunk more than a sip or two of alcohol. I told her, "No thanks, I don't drink." She laughed and said, "Everyone drinks." She proceeded to drink a bottle of beer while we rode around, and I pondered the temptation for a while.

She was having a great time, acting like she did not have a care in the world, flirting, and laughing with every guy that stopped to talk to us. I wanted to feel that free and brave without any restraints. Even though my Christian walk was not strong, I knew that I would feel guilty afterward for drinking. I became envious of her carefree behavior, so I talked myself into having just one beer. To my surprise, I immediately liked the taste and the way it made me feel.

My reserved, shy demeanor was now outgoing and flirty. I enjoyed the attention that I got from guys. As a result, I began drinking on the weekends, and hanging around this much older crowd of friends throughout my high school years. I was developing poor habits. Sure,

I would feel temporary guilt and repent, but soon after I would repeat these same sins. I was unaware that my drinking habits were creating a stronghold that would keep me enslaved in the cycle of habitual sins for many years to come.

Overview

God desires to have a close relationship with us and dwell in our hearts through our faith in Jesus Christ. Unconfessed, habitual sins sever this relationship and keep us from experiencing the fullness and abundance of God. But, the forgiveness of Jesus can renew our minds and transform our hearts when we accept His grace and apply His mercy and love toward ourselves and others. Then, we can grasp the deep love of Christ by practicing Spirit-filled habits.

We are called to abide in Jesus and follow His example of grace by allowing His attributes to shine through us onto others. This kind of light makes it possible to walk in the Spirit (live, serve, and bear fruit). Paul explained in the book of Romans how to be set free from habitual sins and take root or hold of living in the new way of the Spirit.

DAY ONE

The New Way of the Spirit

*"For while we were living in the flesh, our sinful passions, aroused by the law, were at work in our members to bear fruit for death. But now we are released from the law, having died to that which held us captive, so that we serve in the **new way of the Spirit** and not in the old way of the written code (law)"* (Romans 7:5 – 6, ESV).

By being aware of the law, we may feel rebellious or condemned by the law because of our sinful nature. Since the law does not justify us, we look to Jesus to teach us how to live in the new way of the Spirit. We find these instructions in the Scriptures because it is the holy, inspired Word of God.

The Word is used to teach us what is true, noble, pure, right, and make us aware of our (habitual) sins so that the Holy Spirit can help us choose to do what is pleasing and right before the Lord. Paul discovered that only by the grace of God, through Jesus Christ our Lord, he has the power to overcome his habitual sins and the strength to put on the full armor of God every single day.

When this act of surrender occurs, the Holy Spirit can reveal the deeper things of God to us. Therefore, when the Spirit reveals these revelations to us, we have a desire to *live, serve, and bear fruit* in the new way of the Spirit.

Live in the New Way of the Spirit

"Therefore, there is now no condemnation for those who are in Christ Jesus, who do not walk according to the flesh, but according to the Spirit" (Romans 8:1, NKJV).

There are a few phrases that I still remember my grandmother saying when I was a child. The one that sticks out the most is, "Walk in the Spirit and truth." Now, as a child, I had no idea what she meant by this phrase. I just knew it was a good thing and something I should strive to do. The question remained: exactly how am I supposed to do this? I felt like Paul when he said, *"For I know that nothing good dwells in me, that is, in my flesh. For I have the desire to do what is right, but not the ability to carry it out"* (*Romans 7:18, ESV*). He was right! We cannot live in the new way of the Spirit by carrying it out in our own strength.

The mind of the flesh and the Spirit are in constant battle. We cannot serve two masters. We will either love the one or hate the other. The mind of the flesh does not appreciate the deeper things of God. The flesh desires to be selfish, self-centered, arrogant, prideful, immoral, and greedy—you name it—no good thing dwells in our flesh.

The Scriptures instruct us not to gratify the desires of the flesh but to focus our mind on the heavenly things above. *"For those who live according to the flesh set their minds on the things of the flesh, but those who live according to the Spirit set their minds on the things of the Spirit. For to set the mind on the flesh is death, but to set the mind on the Spirit is life and peace" (Romans 8:5 – 6, ESV).*

Therefore, God promises to give us a new mind, a new heart, and a new spirit once we surrender and commit our lives to Him. The *new-self* desires to live according to the Spirit and have a relationship with God. When we focus on the deeper things of God, we can develop spirit-filled habits. As we practice these new habits, (become rooted and grounded in Christ) the desire or need to live in the new way of the Spirit is much stronger than the need to gratify the desires of the flesh. When dying to the flesh occurs, we can now serve in the new way of the Spirit.

Complete Day 1 – Workbook Activity (optional)

DAY TWO

Serve in the New Way of the Spirit

"Then Jesus said to his disciples, "If any of you wants to be my follower, you must give up your own way, take up your cross, and follow me. If you try to hang on to your (old) life, you will lose it. But if you give up your (old) life for my sake, you will save it" (Matthew 16:24 – 25, NLT).

If living in the Spirit is a new habit, then serving in the Spirit is a lifestyle. We take up our cross daily, surrender our will, and have a desire to do God's will, instead of our own. We are not under the condemnation and regulations of the religious laws, but free to serve in the new way of the Spirit who dwells within us. Paul said, *"Where the Spirit of the Lord is, there is freedom"* (*2 Corinthians 3:17, ESV*).

Paul and the early church were no longer under the Old Testament covenant when sacrificial lambs were slain to shed blood for the forgiveness of sins. They and we are forgiven and free from the bondage of sin when we accept Christ as our Savior. *"For God did not give us a spirit of fear, but of power, love, and self-control"* (*2 Timothy 1:7, WEB*).

How do we serve in the new way of the Spirit? Paul's answer is by the gift of grace. *"But by the grace of God I am what I am, and his grace to me was not without effect. No, I worked harder than all of them—yet not I, but the grace of God that was with me"* (*I Corinthians 15:10*).

Paul longed to grow in the fullness of God's grace. He knew there was more to life and being a Christian after his conversion or salvation experience. He also knew serving in the new way of the Spirit gave him a desire for prayer, to know God's will, and to have a relationship with Him. Paul traveled and worked hard to preach and spread the gospel of grace to all the nations. Paul trusted and had faith in God's grace to sustain him and the Holy Spirit to guide him on all his missionary journeys.

Another phrase my grandmother would say is "Be sensitive to the Holy Spirit." I understand now what she meant by that, which is to be mindful, prayerful, and listen to what the Spirit has to say. God said not to conform to this world but to become transformed by the renewing of your mind.

Serving in the new way of the Spirit requires the daily renewal of our mind by reading the Word of God, praying, meditating, and listening to the still small voice of the Holy Spirit to guide us. When we are sensitive to the Holy Spirit, this enables us to become sensitive to the prayer needs of others and gives us a desire to *bear fruit* in the new way of the Spirit.

Complete Day 2 – Workbook Activity (optional)

DAY THREE

Bear Fruit in the New Way of the Spirit

"Abide in me, and I in you. As the branch cannot bear fruit by itself, unless it abides in the vine, neither can you, unless you abide in me" (John 15:4, ESV).

When we listen to the still small voice of the Holy Spirit to guide us, we are indeed abiding in the vine of Christ's love for us. When we are grounded in Christ's love, we have a desire to bear fruit in the new way of the Spirit for Him. This desire is instilled within us by the Holy Spirit to share with others the same love and grace that Christ has shown to us. God wants us to be the branch so He can be the vine and extend Christ's love to others through us.

Therefore, the branch cannot bear fruit alone. It must depend on the vine for nourishment, endurance, and strength. This abiding faith in Christ produces in us mercy, forgiveness, and an unconditional love toward others so we can bear witness and fruit for the Lord. The Spirit desires this for us because God is glorified and magnified through the making of His disciples.

The most puzzling phrase that my grandmother would say was, "Don't grieve the Holy Spirit." Paul stated it in this way, _"And do not grieve the Holy Spirit of God, with whom you were sealed for the day of redemption. Get rid of all bitterness, rage, and anger, brawling and slander, along with every form of malice"_ (Ephesians 4:30-31).

Since grief is a feeling, the Holy Spirit has a great desire and love for us to live in the righteousness of Jesus. It grieves the Spirit when we choose to live in sin and wrong others. The Holy Spirit wants to walk alongside us, guide us, and dwell in us to protect us from sin and self-destruction.

After Jesus's resurrection, He sent the gift of the Holy Spirit to be a Helper and a Comforter to us. Once we are born again, Jesus breathes the Holy Spirit into our hearts and minds to help us live a pleasing and righteous (sanctifying) life before God. The Holy Spirit helps us to say and do the right things, to be an encouragement to others, and to bear fruit for the Lord.

Complete Day 3 – Workbook Activity (optional)

DAY FOUR

Our sinful, rebellious nature wants to reject the will of God because of our selfish desire to do and get what we want all the time. For in Paul's strength (flesh) he could not do what his mind and heart wanted, which was to honor and follow God's will and live a pleasing life before Him.

He could not conquer or die to sin in his strength. Only Christ could conquer sin by taking our place and dying on the cross so we could inherit eternal life. But, until that eternal day, habitual sins can still sever our relationship with God and lead to spiritual bondage on this earth.

What habitual sins are keeping you from living, serving, and bearing fruit in the new way of the Spirit? Complete the comparison chart by replacing the habits of the old self with the spirit-filled habits of the new self.

Habitual Sins (Old Self)   **Spirit-filled Habits (New Self)**

$\longrightarrow$

Complete Day 4 – Workbook Activity (optional)

DAY FIVE
Reflection

What does it mean when Jesus says, "my yoke is easy, and my burden is light?"[3]

Adapted from:
https://www.gotquestions.org/yoke-easy-burden-light.html

Answer: The saying "my yoke is easy, and my burden is light" is part of a larger passage (Matthew 11:28–30), in which Jesus tells all who are weary and burdened to come to Him for rest. He isn't speaking here of physical difficulties. Rather, it was the heavy burden of the system of works (laws) that the Pharisees laid on the backs of the people that Jesus was offering to relieve. Later on, in Matthew's Gospel, Jesus will rebuke the Pharisees for laying heavy burdens on the shoulders of the people (Matthew 23:4).

The "yoke of the Pharisees" is the burdensome yoke of **self-righteousness and legalistic law-keeping**. Biblical scholars have said that the Pharisees added 600 regulations regarding what qualified as "working" on the Sabbath. That is a heavy burden! Recall the story of the lawyer who asked Jesus what the greatest commandment of the Law was (Matthew 22:36). You can almost read between the lines of the man's question: "What law, of all the laws we have, do I absolutely have to keep?"

Jesus was saying that any law-keeping is burdensome and amounts to a "heavy yoke" of oppression because no amount of law-keeping can bridge the gap between our sinfulness and God's holiness. God says through the mouth of the prophet Isaiah that all of our righteous deeds are like a "polluted garment," and Paul reiterated to the Romans that "no one will be declared righteous in his sight by observing the law" (Romans 3:20).

The good news is that Jesus promises to all who come to Him that He will give them rest from the heavy burden of trying to

Come to Me, all you who labor and are heavy laden, and I will give you rest. Take My yoke upon you and learn from Me, for I am gentle and lowly in heart, and you will find rest for your soul.

For My *Yoke* is easy and My burden is *light*.

Matthew 11:28-30 (ESV)

earn our way into heaven and rest from the oppressive yoke of self-righteousness and legalism. Jesus encourages those who are "heavy laden" to take His yoke upon them, and in so doing they will find rest for their souls.

The yoke of Jesus is light and easy to carry because it is the yoke of repentance and faith followed by a singular commitment to follow Him. As the apostle, John says, "For this is the love of God, that we keep his commandments. And his commandments are not burdensome" (1 John 5:3).

Jesus says in Matthew 11:30, "His yoke is easy and His burden light." Now, we might think that there is no difference between the commandments of Jesus and the Jewish Law. Isn't the same God responsible for both? Technically speaking, yes. If anything, one might argue that the commands of Jesus are even more burdensome because **His reformulation of the Mosaic Law in the Sermon on the Mount** (Matthew 5—7) goes above and beyond a mere outward conformity to the Law and deals instead with the **inner person**.

What makes Jesus's yoke easy and His burden light is that in Jesus's **active obedience** (i.e., His perfect fulfillment of the Law of God), He carried the burden that we were meant to carry. His **perfect obedience** is applied (imputed) to us through **faith,** just as His righteousness was exchanged for our sin at the cross (2 Corinthians 5:21).

Our obedience to Jesus then becomes our "spiritual worship" (Romans 12:1). Furthermore, we are indwelt by the Holy Spirit who works in our lives to mold us into the image of Christ, thereby making the yoke of Jesus easy and His burden light. The life lived by **faith is a much lighter yoke and a much easier burden to carry than the heavy and burdensome yoke of self-righteousness** under which some continually strive to make themselves acceptable to God through works.

Complete Day 5 – Workbook Activity (optional)

Week 2

WITH ALL MY HEART

The Thorn in my Heart: Pride

As a young adult on my way to college, my older friends were no longer an influence on me. But, my earlier learned behaviors and habitual sins became instilled in my heart. I chose to follow these habits and give them a stronghold over my life.

In college, I joined a sorority and instantly had a slew of friends to hang out and drink with on a regular basis. This time I was not living in my parents' home, so I not only drank every weekend, but I began going to parties and drinking two or three times during the week. When we had a fraternity drop-in on a Tuesday or Wednesday night, the sorority sisters were required to make an appearance, and there was always plenty of alcohol on hand.

I grew up in a town of about 7,500 people. College life was fun, exciting, and there were more guys in college than in my hometown. During homecoming week, I met a fraternity guy that was a junior and became obsessed with getting his attention. I flirted with him at parties and thought about him all the time.

My sorority had a formal coming up. It was customary for girls to invite guys to their formals. I didn't know this guy, but

Christ will live in your *hearts* because of your *faith*. Stand firm and be deeply *rooted in his love*.

Ephesians 3:17 (CEV)

I took a chance and invited him. He said, yes. I was ecstatic. I called one of my friends from high school to borrow her blue suede dress and shoes. I picked up the items the weekend before the formal.

The night arrived. I was nervous about my date, but before long the alcohol began to flow on the chartered bus. I became flirty and fun. We danced, laughed, and had a good time with our friends. As the night grew long, he and I became more inebriated.

After the formal, he drove me to his frat house where he lived. We began making out on his bed. He reached down to slip his hands up my dress and under my panties. I gasped and whispered in his ear, "wait…I'm still a virgin." At that moment, I thought he would get mad and kick me out of his room. To my surprise, he had the biggest grin on his face. He said, it's okay and proceeded to rub with his hand. I felt a sense of fear and warmth all at the same time. It was the first time someone had touched me there since I was four years old.

As intoxicated as I was, I immediately decided it was not going any further, and it didn't. Luckily for me, we both eventually passed out and slept until the morning. When I woke up, I was sobered and embarrassed. We didn't talk about the evening at all. In fact, I called one of my sorority sisters to pick me up and asked her to bring me a change of clothes.

I wasn't about to leave that fraternity house in the same dress that I wore the night before. He went downstairs to get the clothes from my friend; he brought the clothes to me, and I changed in his room while he found something to eat. Shoes, I thought? Where are the tennis shoes? There I was in shorts, a t-shirt, and a pair of high-heeled blue suede shoes.

My friend was waiting for me outside in her car (we didn't have cell phones back then). I cleared my throat, opened the door to his room and took the walk of shame down the hall past several frat guys. Then, I flew down the stairs, past some more guys, and walked right out the front door of the frat house and jumped into my friend's car.

I felt like such a loser, disgusted with myself, and fortunate the evening did not turn into something much worse. The next weekend I saw him at the dorm picking up some other girl for a date, so that was the end of my obsession with him.

I cannot remember attending church at all my freshman year of college unless it was an important holiday or the one day a year the fraternities and sororities participated in a church service together. Greek life became a way of life. I spent my time at frat parties, intramural games, meetings, and any Greek social that I was required to attend.

I made a 1.6 GPA my first semester, lost my scholarship, and felt like a total failure. My parents said to take out a student loan or come home because they were not paying for me to major in partying. So, I took out a student loan, received a grant, and found a part-time waitress job to cover my expenses.

During my second semester, I was on sorority probation for my grades and required to attend study sessions in the dorm suite every week. I still went to parties and had fun, but I learned how to manage my time, attend classes, study, and become a serious student. My GPA was a three-point something the next semester; I got off of sorority probation, found a part-time job at a daycare, but was still drinking during the week and every weekend with my friends.

Sophomore year, I invited a sorority sister to move into a rented house with another girl and me. She was a good Catholic girl; she had a serious boyfriend, and most importantly, she didn't drink. I wasn't dating or even interested. I didn't want to get sidetracked any further. I was focused on accomplishing my goals and not letting distractions detour me on my path to success.

I was pretty skinny at this time. One roommate asked me if I was anorexic because she never saw me eat. My answer was "No. I'm just broke." I had gotten a new job working at a Montessori after-school program in my field of study, was feeling productive and good about myself.

In my third year, I became bored and tired of the party scene. In my heart, I knew there was more to college and life than drinking. I became friends with a guy who taught the singles and university class at his church. He was also active in the Baptist Student Union (BSU) on campus. I'll call him "McDreamy" from Grey's Anatomy.

He invited me to his Sunday school class, church services, and the BSU. I developed a crush on him, which motivated me even more to attend these events so I could see him.

I was meeting new people and developing a positive social circle to surround myself with to reinforce my new perspective. I was achieving my educational goals and working towards my career goals. I felt responsible and could see the light at the end of this college tunnel.

McDreamy was an alumnus of a fraternity and invited me to go with him to the Homecoming Game. I wore my best red dress, red lipstick, and black heels to represent the school colors. I was so proud to be his date. We attended a gathering at his fraternity house before the big game.

As we left the house to walk to the field, a cute blonde motioned him to the side to have a few words with him. After about five minutes of standing solo, I decided to walk to the field alone. He caught up with me and apologized. My brave self, or perhaps the liquid courage, asked him if he wanted to take that blonde to the game, instead of me. He said, "No, I asked you, didn't I?" I said, well, yes and left it at that.

When we arrived at the field, we sat with his best friend and some other people. Less than ten minutes later, McDreamy vanished for the entire game. His best friend was kind and gracious enough to sit with me during the game, or maybe he just felt sorry for me. Either way, McDreamy mysteriously reappeared when the game was over. I invited him to my sorority formal in February, but that was our last date.

In late April, my roommate wanted to introduce me to a guy that was friends with her boyfriend. I told her that I wasn't interested in meeting or dating anyone and we forgot about it. But, one night her boyfriend and his friend "unexpectedly" stopped by the house. This friend was tall, lean, brown-haired with green eyes, and a charming smile to match his witty demeanor. Let's just say, I was in trouble.

I made sure that I was not overly flirty, too friendly, or even acted remotely interested in him. We all sat on the couches and had a nice, cordial conversation. I mentioned that I was in the process of packing and moving into a house with some girls from the BSU and in need of more boxes.

Of course, this fella offered to find and bring me more boxes and even help load them into my car. Yes, prince charming said he would bring them over the next day. He asked when would be a good time to do so.

After they had left, I thought, wow, he sure was nice but just a little too assertive for my taste. I talked myself out of liking him and made sure this was not going any further than packing and loading up boxes. Boy, I was wrong.

For the sake of confidentiality purposes, I will call this guy Jake Ryan. Yes, the actor from the 1984 movie *Sixteen Candles*, because he was just as cute. I made it known to Jake that I was not interested in having a dating relationship with anyone and did not want to have a boyfriend, which made him pursue me even more.

If I told him that I was going to the library to study, he'd show up at the library. If I went to the gym to exercise, there he was. He was unrelenting in his pursuit of me. I didn't find it scary or creepy. I was flattered, enjoyed his attention, and the feeling of being desired.

I told Jake about the church that I attended. He and his best friend started attending this church and the singles class. Jake shared an apartment with his best friend. I found myself over at their place almost every evening to eat dinner with them. I was no longer starving, and it's never been too difficult to entice me with food.

Jake and I became friends. We spent our spare time together and eventually became an item. Jake did not drink alcohol, so I was sober the two years that we dated. I was still adamant about calling all the shots in our relationship. I made sure every aspect of the relationship was on my terms.

During my fourth year of college, I was still living in a house with the girls, who were actively involved in the BSU. I tried out for and made the BSU drama team. I was traveling to different churches in the area to perform with this team. I enjoyed spending time with my new friends.

I even saved enough money to go on a mission trip to Jamaica with 25 other BSU college students. I was content, focused, involved in church, and had a steady boyfriend. I was even elected by my sorority to be the Keeper of the Ritual that year. I was in *my* Christian flow.

The first year of dating Jake was great, but during my fifth year of college, I became clingy and dependent on him to make me happy. I became increasingly selfish and self-absorbed in my relationship with him. I insisted that meeting all of my needs and my wants should always come first. I noticed he was becoming distant and uninterested in the relationship, which made me even more desperate for his time and attention.

I declared alumni status in the sorority that spring semester so I could focus on my student teaching and spend my spare time with him. I was so preoccupied with my studies and completing my degree I hardly noticed that Jake was unhappy and eventually we were spending less time together. In May, after I graduated with a BSE in teaching, my boyfriend of two years broke up with me.

I was devastated, depressed, and heartbroken to learn that Jake had found someone new. I had my college diploma in one hand, no job offers in the other, and no boyfriend on my arm. I was anxious to find a teaching job to support myself. I only applied for teaching positions that would allow me to relocate from the area.

It was mid-July. I still had no offers for a public-school job. Finally, I received a call from a principal to interview for a teaching position in an adjoining state. I drove two hours for an interview. The next week, the principal called and offered me the job. I was moving to a new state, starting my first full-time teaching job, and getting a fresh start.

WEEK 2 – The Mystery of God
Paul's Letter to the Ephesians 1 – 3

Overview

In the first part of the letter, Paul advised the Ephesians to have a continual spirit of thankfulness for everything God had done for them through Jesus Christ. Paul revealed the mystery of God's will and eternal plan (the new covenant) for all people, both the Jews and

Gentiles.

The *mystery of God's will* is that *all believers* in Jesus are members and united into one body of Christ, the Church. The separation of Jews and Gentiles by the Law no longer existed. The old covenant was replaced with a new one to join all believers into the Church. Paul prayed the Ephesians would fully know the *hope they have in Christ*, *the riches of His glorious inheritance* (eternal life), and *the greatness of His power* that is in those who believe.

DAY ONE

<u>Spiritual Blessings in Christ</u>
Ephesians 1:1 – 6

"Praise be to the God and Father of our Lord Jesus Christ, who has blessed us in the heavenly realms with every spiritual blessing in Christ. For *He* chose us in *Him* before the creation of the world to be holy and blameless in *His* sight. In love *He* predestined us for adoption to sonship through Jesus Christ, in accordance with *His* pleasure and will— to the praise of *His* glorious grace, which *He* has freely given us in the One *He* loves."

Paul told the Ephesians that they are born and adopted as children into the beloved family of God. The Spirit of sonship (being a child of God) includes not only *justification* and spiritual blessings, but also the *transformational* opportunity to experience *sanctification* (to be set apart or holy), and have a loving personal relationship with the Father through His Son, Jesus Christ.[4]

<u>The Mystery of God's Will and Eternal Plan</u>
Ephesians 1:7 – 12

Paul said the *mystery of God's will* is that in Christ alone, through His sacrifice and death on the cross, we have redemption through His blood and the forgiveness of sins, in accordance with the riches of God's grace that He lavished on us. With all wisdom and understanding, God gave His Son to die for our sins as an extension of His great mercy, grace, and steadfast love.

According to His eternal plan, all believers, both the Jews and Gentiles, will inherit and be united in the kingdom of God for the praise of His glory. "The Cross eradicated every trace of hostility between God and humanity, and through Jesus's blood and broken body, we are all made one. In Christ, men and women are one flesh. In Christ, Jews and Gentiles are woven into one vine. In Christ, the Old Testament and New Testament saints become one cloud of witnesses."[5]

The Guarantee of our Inheritance
Ephesians 1:13 – 17

Paul said those who heard the word of truth, the gospel of salvation, trusted, and believed in Christ are guaranteed God's redemption and inheritance. They have this promise through the resurrection and glorification of Jesus Christ. He seals the promise with the gift and assurance of the Holy Spirit in their lives.

Paul was prayerful and thankful for the evidence of the Ephesians' faith and their love for all the believers in the body of Christ. He also prayed God would give them a spirit of wisdom and the revelation to know and understand everything God had given and done for them through Jesus.

Head of All Things
Ephesians 1:18 – 23

Paul prayed that God would open the spiritual eyes of the Ephesians' hearts. He prayed they would fulfill the hope of God's calling on earth and in heaven. He said there is nothing compared to the glory of His riches and inheritance.

Paul prayed for the Ephesians to realize that the very same power that raised Jesus from the dead is the very same power living in all believers. This same power resurrected and seated Jesus at the right hand of the Father. This power raised Him far above and over all principalities or enemies in heaven, on earth, and in the world to come.

Therefore, God placed **all things** under the feet of Jesus and made Him the head of **all things**, including the church which is His body. Christ not only fills the church and the community of believers with His presence, but **all things** in the universe will have a revelation of His power, wisdom, and glory through the body of Christ, the Church.

Paul's Prayer to the Ephesians for Enlightenment

[18] *"I pray that the eyes of your heart may be enlightened in order that you may know the **hope** to which he has called you, the **riches** of his glorious inheritance in his holy people,* [19] *and his incomparably great **power** for us who believe. That power is the same as the mighty strength* [20] *he exerted when he raised Christ from the dead and seated him at his right hand in the heavenly realms,* [21] *far above all rule and authority, power and dominion, and every name that is invoked, not only in the present age but also in the one to come.* [22] *And God placed **all things under his feet** and appointed him to be head over everything for the church,* [23] *which is his body, the fullness of him who fills everything in every way."*

Complete Day 1 – Workbook Activity (optional)

DAY TWO

Reconciliation to God through Faith in Jesus Christ
Ephesians 2:1 – 7

Paul told the Ephesians that they were once spiritually dead in their sins and trespasses, but now they are made alive and saved by God's grace. In their trespasses, they pushed the boundaries of God because of the rebellious, sinful nature they inherited from Adam.

Paul advised them not to walk according to Satan, who influences them to have a spirit of disobedience toward God. This kind of spirit desires to fulfill the lusts of the mind and flesh because by nature we are all children of wrath. We deserve God's wrath, but instead, God raised us up with Christ and seated us with Him (co-heirs) in the heavenly realms, in order to show the riches of His grace, expressed in His kindness to us in Christ.

The Gift of Salvation – our New Identity *in Christ*
Ephesians 2:8 – 13

Paul told the Ephesians, "*For by grace you have been saved through faith.*" They could not save themselves; salvation is a gift from God and not earned by works so that no one can boast. Therefore, God receives the glory for salvation and not humankind because they are His creation. *"For we are God's handiwork, created in Christ Jesus to do good works, which God prepared in advance for us to do."*

Paul said God not only saves us but transforms us by His love into a new creation in Jesus Christ (2 Cor. 5:17). As evidence of this transformation, we are called to walk by faith in Jesus to accomplish His good works.

At one time, the Gentiles were without hope in Christ, without God, and without the commonwealth and privileges of the Jews to worship in the temple, claim spiritual blessings, and the old covenant promises. But now *in Christ*, the Gentiles have been reconciled to God by the sacrificial death and love of His Son. "*But now in Christ Jesus, you who once were far away have been brought near by the blood of Christ.*"

The Gift of the Church
Ephesians 2:14 – 18

Jesus is our peace and salvation for both the Jews and Gentiles. Jesus broke down the barrier of conflict, the wall of hostility between these two groups. The hostility being that the Jews had the covenant promise and followed the Law, whereas, the Gentiles did not. But Jesus paid the penalty for the Jews failure to keep the Law *"by setting aside in His flesh the law with its commands and regulations"* and reconciling them both *"to God through the cross, by which he put to death their hostility"* and brought them together into one body, the Church.

His purpose was to create in Himself one new humanity out of the two, thus making peace. Jesus came to earth, preached peace, and died for the sins of all—the Gentiles and Jews. For through Christ, both are reconciled to the Father by One Spirit. "That is why God has given us the Spirit that now resides in our hearts. It is so that we can be holy, set apart, and reflect the holy nature of God—Himself. We are a public witness to all of humanity."[6]

Complete Day 2 – Workbook Activity (optional)

DAY THREE

<u>The Foundation of the Church</u>
Ephesians 2:19 – 22

Paul explained how the Jews and Gentiles were no longer strangers and foreigners, but fellow heirs with all believers and equal members of the family of God. He said we are all under the body of Christ and receive the same grace and promises of God.

Paul said to build upon the foundation laid by the apostles and prophets, *"with Christ Jesus himself as the chief cornerstone. In Him, the whole building is joined together and rises to become a holy temple in the Lord. And in Him, you too are being built together to become a dwelling in which God lives by his Spirit."*

<u>One Body of Christ</u>
Ephesians 3:1 – 6

Paul said he was a prisoner of Jesus Christ on behalf of the Gentiles and not a prisoner of man. Paul, being falsely accused, was arrested in Jerusalem for bringing a Gentile into the Jewish temple. Paul and the Gentile Christians believed that God had called him (Paul) to preach the gospel to them and reveal the revelation of God's mystery.

God brought the believing Gentiles together with the Jews to form one body of Christ, one Church. The mystery of God's plan for the church was not made known to man in the Old Testament. By the grace of God, Paul was used as an instrument to explain how the two would unite into one Church. The believing Gentiles would no longer be separated, but fellow heirs with the Jews and partakers of God's new covenant promise in Christ through the gospel.

<u>Fellow Heirs</u>
Ephesians 3:7 – 12

Paul became a servant of the gospel by the gift of God's grace given to him through the power of God. Paul said even though he was the very least deserving of all the apostles, this grace was given to him to teach the Gentiles. He taught on the boundless riches of Christ and made plain to everyone the purpose of this mystery, which for ages past was kept hidden in God, who created all things. *"His intent was that now, through the church, the manifold wisdom of God should be made known to the rulers and authorities in the heavenly realms, according to His eternal purpose that He accomplished in Christ Jesus our Lord."*

"Ephesians 3:10 is one of the clearest in all of Paul's writings telling us that our redemption is ultimately for the purpose of making the glory of the Lord known to His creation. We see that the creation of the Church through the preaching of the gospel is designed to proclaim the *manifold wisdom* of God." [7]

Therefore, God reveals His manifold wisdom through the workings of the church. Paul desired for the Ephesians to fellowship in the great riches of Christ's crucifixion, resurrection, and the new covenant promise that reconciliation to God is available to *all believers* through their faith in Jesus Christ. Henceforth, all believers can pray directly with boldness to access the throne room of God. *"In him and through faith in him, we may approach God with freedom and confidence."*

Complete Day 3 – Workbook Activity (optional)

DAY FOUR

Prayer for Strength
Ephesians 3:13 – 19

Paul said his sufferings were for the sake of spreading the gospel of grace. Even though Paul was imprisoned in Rome, God was still using him for His glory. While under house arrest, Paul wrote letters to the Ephesians, the Colossians, the Philippians, and to Philemon.

Paul was humble and understood God's will and purpose for his life. With a **heart of humility**, he wrote this prayer for the Ephesians to strengthen their faith in God, their love for one another, and their hope by uniting as one body of Christ through the Church.

*[14] For this reason, I kneel before the Father, [15] from whom every family in heaven and on earth derives its name. [16] I pray that out of His glorious riches He may strengthen you with power through His Spirit in your inner being, [17] so that Christ may dwell in your hearts through faith. And I pray that you, being **rooted and grounded** in love, [18] may have **power**, together with all the Lord's holy people, to grasp how wide and long and high and deep is the love of Christ, [19] and to know this love that surpasses knowledge—that you may be filled to the measure of all the fullness of God.*

The Fullness of God
Ephesians 3:20 – 21

"Now to him who is able to do immeasurably more than all we ask or imagine, according to his power that is at work within us, to him be glory

May your *roots* go down deep into the soil of God's *marvelous love*. And may you have the *power* to *understand*, as all God's people should, how wide, how long, how high, and how deep *His love* really is.

Ephesians 3:17-18 (NLT)

in the church and in Christ Jesus throughout all generations, for ever and ever! Amen."

As believers, we do not have to wait until eternity to access the resurrection power of Jesus. Paul proclaimed that the attributes of spiritual strength, blessings, wisdom, the heart of Christ, and the fullness of God belong to all believers **now** *according to his power that is at work within us.*

Paul desired for them to experience the power, love, and fullness of God – the abundant life in Christ. He prayed the Ephesians would grasp just *how wide and long and high and deep is the love of Christ* for them.

Complete Day 4 – Workbook Activity (optional)

DAY FIVE
Reflection

Paul's Sufferings for the Sake of Christ

Paul said, "Five times I received from the Jews the forty lashes minus one. Three times I was beaten with rods, once I was pelted with stones, three times I was shipwrecked, I spent a night and a day in the open sea, I have constantly been on the move. I have been in danger from rivers, in danger from bandits, in danger from my fellow Jews, in danger from Gentiles; in danger in the city, in danger in the country, in danger at sea; and in danger from false believers. I have labored, and toiled and have often gone without sleep; I have known hunger and thirst and have often gone without food; I have been cold and naked. Besides everything else, I face daily the pressure of my concern for all the churches. Who is weak, and I do not feel weak? Who is led into sin, and I do not inwardly burn? If I must boast, I will boast of the things that show my weakness" (2 Corinthians 11:24 – 30).

Paul knew what it meant to suffer for the sake of Christ. He also understood that suffering was for God's glory and his good. *"Yet what we suffer now (present time) is nothing compared to the glory he will reveal to us later" (Romans 8:18, NLT).*

In Paul's prayer to the Ephesians for enlightenment, verses 1:18 – 23, he encourages them to persevere despite their present circumstances so that they may <u>KNOW the **hope** to which God has called them</u>. He said these sufferings or trials are preparing us for that time when He will reveal His glory to us. Paul said all of these trials are working together for our good, for those called according to His purpose (Romans 8:28).

Paul prayed the Ephesians would <u>KNOW the **riches** of His glorious inheritance in His holy people</u>. Paul said the Christian life should never be complacent, narrow, or rigid. God has an exciting adventure waiting for those who make themselves available to be used by Him. We make ourselves available to God when we give Him our life and trust Him in every situation.

Therefore, we surrender our life and circumstances to God in the good times and the bad. *"Do not conform to the pattern of this world, but be transformed by the renewing of your mind. Then you will be able to test and approve what God's will is—his good, pleasing and perfect will" (Romans 12:2, NIV).*

Paul prayed the Ephesians would <u>KNOW the **greatness** of His power that is in those who believe</u>. Paul said the same power that raised Jesus from the dead is the same everlasting power living in you and me. *"For God did not give us a spirit of fear, but of power and love, and a sound mind" (2 Timothy 1:7, NHEB).* Resurrection power has no fear; it casts its cares or burdens upon the Lord, and works best and glorifies God in our weaknesses. God wants you to surrender and cast your cares and sins upon Him so that His power can be made perfect in your weakness.

Complete Day 5 – Workbook Activity (optional)

[8]Adapted from Stedman, Ray C. "Hope, Riches, and Power (*Ephesians 1:18-23*)."

...to be *made new* in the attitude of your minds; and to put on the *new self*, created to be *like God* in true righteousness and *holiness.*

Ephesians 4:23-24 NIV

Week 3

WITH ALL MY MIND

The Thorn in My Mind — Rebellion

The summer after graduating from college, I relocated to another state, moved into an apartment, and started my teaching career. I was feeling self-sufficient but still depressed over the breakup with Jake. The apartment complex I lived in housed other teachers who worked at the same elementary school with me.

We commuted together, hung out at one another's apartments, religiously watched our favorite TV shows each week, made classroom materials together, and went to happy hour at the local bar every week after work. It didn't take long for my old drinking ways to resurface. Happy hour was my time to vent, complain, and gripe about my rough day at work and reinforce my drinking habits.

Our group quickly extended to male friends once we started bar hopping on the weekends. We met some guys who just graduated from college and were starting their first career, as well. Our group was growing, and we all had one thing in common that we learned and majored in at college – social drinking. My old habit and my new friends were a perfect match. We enjoyed partying during the week, the weekends, and going to bars or clubs. God was nowhere on my radar screen.

The two years that I lived there, I may have attended church a handful of times or less. My focus was on easing the pain of my breakup and surrounding myself with a new set of friends who liked to party and drink as much as I did. Social drinking is how I filled my time and the void in my heart.

Reflecting back, I can see how I alienated myself from God. I excused, justified, and blamed my poor decisions and behaviors on my circumstances, rather than seeking God's wisdom and will for my life. I understand now why it is so important to pray, protect your mind, and guard your heart against the temptations of sin, especially during tough times, because the flesh is weak.

Even if the spirit is willing to choose wisely, when you surround yourself with temptation it is easy to convince yourself that it is okay to have one more drink, to gossip, to hurt the person who hurt you or engage in hateful behaviors. Over the years, I put my faith, hope, and trust in alcohol to fulfill, sustain, and comfort me during the most difficult times in my life.

But, I learned that Jesus has a much better plan for me. He wants me to set my mind on the things above and the hope of His glory and grace. My grandmother used to say, "Sin separates you from God." I understand, now, she meant that sin severs your relationship with God. Unfortunately, I had to learn the hard way, but now I have gratitude for God's mercy and grace for sending His son as a provision for me. Jesus's love covers a multitude of sins (past, present, and future).

This mindset inspired my purpose for writing about Paul's experiences and sharing my own. I want to help others, like myself, understand how the trap of habitual sins keeps us from walking in freedom and forgiveness, living out our faith in Jesus, and experiencing the abundant life that God intends for all of His children to have.

It was mid-May and the completion of my second year of teaching. I had just finished my third semester of graduate school in the field of counseling. I attended graduate school part-time in the evenings while teaching full-time during the day.

It was the end of the school year for the students. The principal asked to speak with me as the last bell rang and the children left the building for their summer break. I walked into his office. He shut the door. He walked over to sit behind his desk. I sat opposite of him in a metal cushioned chair. I had no idea what we were meeting about so I sat there and listened to him speak.

He told me that he and the school board decided not to renew my contract for a third year. He said August would be my last paycheck. I gulped and stared at him in silent disbelief. He thanked me for my service and asked if I had any questions. With a frozen stare, I looked him in the eyes and said, "I do not have any questions." He stood up, I stood up, we shook hands, and I left his office. As I walked back to my classroom, I tried to wrap my mind around what had just happened.

I opened my classroom door and sat behind my desk to contemplate my next move for the following half-hour. Three colleagues, who I had become good friends with, came into my classroom. They asked me why I wasn't at the end of the school year meeting. Before I could utter a word, one friend said, "I just knew it. You're not coming back next year, are you?" I said, no, I am not coming back. Another friend asked, "Where did you get another teaching job?" I looked at all three of my friends' curious faces. I could feel the pride swelling within my heart and said, "I didn't get another teaching job. I am moving to the small University town, where I attend school, to be a graduate assistant while I work on my masters."

Of course, this was an absolute lie, but my pride would not have it any other way. Previously, I had been talking to them about applying for a graduate assistantship but had not taken any measures to do so. This was the first thing that came out of my mouth. I said it so proudly and convincingly that my friends did not even question it.

They congratulated me and asked why I had not told them sooner. I said, "I wanted to tell the principal first before I told anyone else." I explained that I had met with him this afternoon so now I am telling people. The next comment was "great, let's go to happy hour and celebrate." So, we did. And, I definitely felt like having a few drinks.

When I went home that evening, I did not tell a soul about what happened to me at work, especially not my parents. I just could not face their disappointment while trying to deal with my own. I was completely blindsided, devastated, embarrassed, and had not felt this rejected since the breakup with my college boyfriend. I had my pity party and planned my next step.

I had three months of pay left and the summer off. I decided to apply for every teaching job that was close to the University that I attended. While working on my masters in counseling, I met and made friends with a classmate who conducted group therapy full-time at a mental health facility. I did not tell her about my lay off, but she said that her company was hiring, so I applied for a position. I am not sure what happened with the job, but they never called me for an interview.

It was now early July, and none of my leads or teaching interviews had panned out. I was beginning to enter panic mode. Realistically, I knew that I could not afford to live on a graduate assistantship without taking out more loans. I was already paying off a loan for my undergraduate degree and did not want more debt.

I had applied for a teaching position in the small town where I attended graduate school. It was about a 60-mile drive from where I currently lived. I was desperately waiting and wondering if I would hear from them. I was worried, depressed, and jobless but I hid it from my parents, my friends, and God.

A week later I got a call and an interview for the teaching position in the small town that I was wanting. I was nervous because I knew that I had to nail the interview or there'd be no teaching job for me. I was still feeling lousy, self-medicating with alcohol, and consumed with guilt about losing my job. I made excuses and justified my behavior as if I was punishing God, instead of myself.

It was the day of the interview. I was still depressed. I thought that I needed something to help me become more outgoing, happy, and friendly so I could impress these people and land the job. I had an hour drive to convince myself that downing a few beers before going into the interview would do the trick.

When I got a few miles from the primary school, I popped open the first bottle and downed it and then the second one in a matter of minutes. I had a bottle of mouthwash to freshen up with, also part of the plan, to conceal the smell. Now, I was ready. I had a buzz and was feeling very confident in myself, besides I had nothing to lose, except for this job, but my arrogance convinced me that it was mine for the taking.

During the interview, I was funny, charming, they were laughing, and we were all having a great time. Then, a lady from the committee asked me why I was leaving my current job. I told her that I was in graduate school and wanted to relocate to the area to be closer to the University. I told them how wonderful the school and teachers were at my "current" school and how much I had learned from them about teaching.

One of the ladies said, "Well, I know the principal at that school, and he's not easy to work with." Bingo, I thought, maybe she will not call him for a reference. Come to find out later, they did not call him, and they offered me the position by the end of the week.

I told my parents that I was planning to relocate to a new town and work at a primary school to be closer to the University that I attended. My parents did not even know that I was job hunting. They were surprised but happy that I would be teaching and attending graduate school less than two miles from where I lived. I was happy too.

I had just met someone that I was interested in having a relationship with that I met at a bar one weekend near my hometown. I'll call him, "Steve." I was moving, changing careers, and now found myself in a long-distance relationship. To maintain this relationship, I would drive two-hours one way to be with Steve on the weekends.

I did not know a soul in this university town other than my classmates. Most of them were younger than me and went from undergraduate straight into graduate school and had not experienced the full-time world of work, yet. I did not have much in common with them.

Plus, I was too tired from working all day and going to classes during the evening to hang out with anyone. I figured out, by this time, going to bars in a small town where the parents of the kids I taught could recognize me was not a smart idea. I was just glad to have a job and was not interested in the bar or club scene, for now.

Week 3 – The Armor of God
Paul's Letter to the Ephesians 4 – 6

Overview

In the second part of the letter, Paul explained how the Jews and Gentiles could unite as one church and walk in a manner that is worthy of their calling in a spirit of unity. Paul described God's spiritual gifts and the leadership roles in the body of Christ, the characteristics of the new self, and God's purpose for submission.

Paul demonstrated how to put on the full armor of God and use the spiritual weapons to stand against the schemes of the devil and his spiritual armies. Paul said by the power of prayer and the Word of God the battle against the devil is defeated. Christ won the war when he died on the cross and was resurrected to reconcile us to a Holy God.

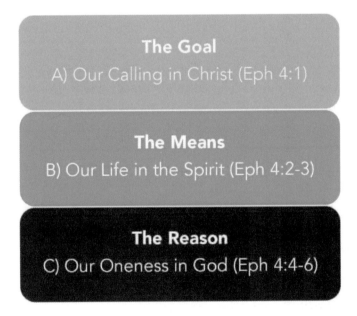

The Goal
A) Our Calling in Christ (Eph 4:1)

The Means
B) Our Life in the Spirit (Eph 4:2-3)

The Reason
C) Our Oneness in God (Eph 4:4-6)

GIFTS OF THE HOLY SPIRIT

DAY ONE

Spiritual Unity
Ephesians 4:1 – 6

Paul explained how to acquire spiritual unity within the church and walk in a manner that is worthy of the calling of Jesus Christ. He said, *"Be completely humble and gentle; be patient, bearing with one another in love. Make every effort to keep the unity of the Spirit through the bond of peace."* Christian humility and gentleness are an attitude of thinking highly of Jesus for what He did while thinking less of ourselves. Therefore, humility leads to bearing with one another in love to create unity and peace in the church.

Paul instructed the Ephesians to ask the Holy Spirit to help them obtain this act of love and maintain unity in the church. Christians have spiritual unity because they all share Jesus in common. In Jesus, there is one body, one spirit, one baptism, and one God, who is over all, through all, and in all.

Spiritual Gifts and Leadership
Ephesians 4:7 – 16

Believers receive spiritual gifts by the grace of God. After the resurrection of Jesus, He gave the body of the church certain gifts. "Through the Holy Spirit, Jesus gave some to be apostles, some prophets, some evangelists, and some pastors and teachers to equip the church for good works of service or ministry."

The *purpose of spiritual gifts* is to build up the body of Christ as we attain the unity of faith, knowledge of the Son of God, and become mature in the fullness and likeness of Jesus. "So, that we may no longer be children, tossed to and fro by the waves and carried about by every wind of doctrine, by human cunning, by craftiness in deceitful schemes." Instead, speak the truth in love and grow in Christ as each part of the body does its work.

THE NEW CREATION MODEL

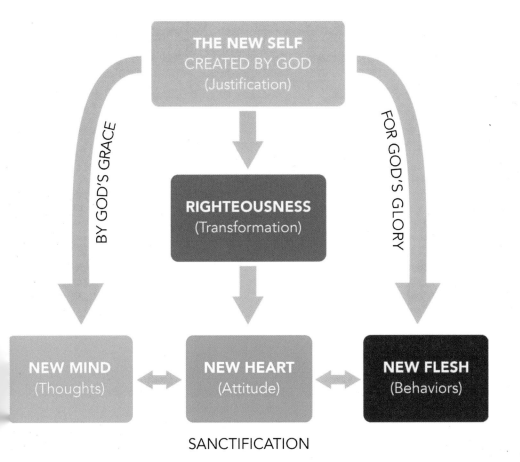

Be *kind* to one another, *tenderhearted*, forgiving one another, just as *God in Christ* forgave you.

Ephesians 4:32 (ESV)

The *New Creation Model* depicts putting on the new self or person, who is created by God's grace. God transforms the new self to be like Jesus to live in true righteousness and holiness. He renews the thoughts of the mind, the attitude of the heart, and the behaviors of the flesh for your sanctification and His glory. *"Therefore, if anyone is in Christ, he or she is a new creation. The old has passed away; behold, the new has come"* (2 Corinthians 5:17, ESV).

Complete Day 1 – Workbook Activity (optional)

DAY TWO

Old Self vs. New Self
Ephesians 4:17 – 24

Paul said we are called to become mature in the fullness and likeness of Christ. We should no longer walk or live like the old self, who lacks understanding and lives in the darkness and futility of the mind, hardens the heart, is alienated from God, and is consumed by the acts of (habitual) sins. Instead, we should live like Christ because the truth is in Jesus.

Therefore, the truth will set us free from futility. *"You were, taught, with regard to your former way of life, to put off your old self, which is being corrupted by its deceitful desires; and to be made new in the attitude of your minds; and to put on the new self, created to be like God in true righteousness and holiness."*

Ephesians 4:25 – 32

Paul said, having put away the old self, let each person speak the truth in love and hold one another accountable. *"In your anger do not sin. Do not let the sun go down while you are still angry, and do not give the devil a foothold."* Anyone who has been stealing, steal no longer.

Instead, do honest labor and help those in need. Put away all bitterness, wrath, clamor, malice, and evil speaking and only speak what is good for edification and imparting grace. And do not grieve the Holy Spirit, whom you received on the day of your salvation, by continuing to engage in (habitual) sins.

Characteristics of the New Self
Ephesians 5:1 – 7

Walk in Love

Paul said, *"Follow God's example, therefore, as dearly loved children."* God's unconditional love towards us is the perfect example of how we should treat one another. The new self walks in love, just as Christ, also loved us and gave Himself as an offering and a pleasing sacrifice to God. We can also give a pleasing sacrifice (a sweet-smelling aroma) to God when we imitate Him, love, and bear witness to others.

Paul mentions the opposite of walking in love is the commitment of sexual sins and impurity, such as fornication, all uncleanness or covetousness, filthiness, foolish talking, and crude joking, which are not fitting for the characteristics of the new self. For such things have no inheritance in the kingdom of God. Therefore, do not be deceived by the acts of disobedience and do not be partakers with those who deserve the wrath of God.

Walk in the Light
Ephesians 5:8 – 17

"For you were once darkness, but now you are light in the Lord." The new self walks in the Spirit – all goodness, righteousness, and truth by practicing behaviors that are acceptable to God. Paul said to avoid the works of darkness, but pray that others will see the light of the Lord in you.

Since you received the light, walk in it wisely and make the most of every opportunity for the glory of Christ because the days are evil. Paul said, *"Therefore do not be foolish, but understand what the Lord's will is."*

Walk in the Spirit
Ephesians 5:18 – 21

Paul said to be careful in how we live, to be wise, and to make the most of every opportunity by bearing witness for Christ. He also contrasts being drunk with being filled with the Holy Spirit. *"Do not get drunk on wine, which leads to debauchery. Instead, be filled with the Spirit, speaking to one another with psalms, hymns, and songs from the Spirit."*

If we consistently practice the spirit-filled habits of the new self, we will have the desire to worship God and pour out His mercy, forgiveness, love, and grace onto others. *"And, remember to give thanks to God always for all things in the name of our Lord Jesus Christ, by submitting to one another out of the utmost respect for the Lord."*

Complete Day 2 – Workbook Activity (optional)

DAY THREE

Walk in Submission
Ephesians 5:22 – 33

The purpose and will of submission are to obey and glorify God. The first act of submission for the new self means recognizing God's sovereignty and behaving accordingly. The second act of submission is for *"Wives, submit yourselves to your own husbands as you do to the Lord."*

I believe this statement means having the right attitude about submission toward your husband and God. This act is done out of obedience and respect for the Lord because He asks this of you. God created Adam and gave him the responsibility to care for Eve. The wife should complement and be a helper to her husband. This is part of her Christian role.

Paul said the husband is the head of the wife, just as Christ is the head of the Church and the Savior of the body. Christ, as the head of the Church loves, nourishes and cherishes the body. He expects the husband to do the same for his wife by taking care of her and presenting her as blameless and spiritually clean before the Lord.

The third reason for submission is for the husband and wife union to model the relationship between Jesus and the Church. The husband is called to leave his father and mother and cleave to his wife as one flesh. He is to love his wife with a self-sacrificing love, the kind in which he would give up his own life for her. He who loves his wife loves himself and let the wife see the wisdom in having respect for her husband.

<u>Parent-Child Relationship</u>
Ephesians 6:1 – 4

Children have the responsibility to obey their parents. This is part of their Christian role. Parents have the privilege to teach their children obedience. Parents accomplish this goal by disciplining their children with love. In effect, this teaches children self-discipline and how to submit to and obey God.

God promises to bring blessings to the children who honor their father and mother. Fathers are instructed, *"Do not exasperate your children; instead, bring them up in the training and instruction of the Lord."* Instead, teach and encourage your children in the Word of God, how to walk in the Lord, and be the example for them.

<u>Employer-Employee Relationship</u>
Ephesians 6:5 – 9

You are to work as if you are working for the Lord with dignity, respect, and a pleasant attitude; not with eyeservice or only working when the employer is watching or only working to please him or her. You are instructed to work from the heart by doing good will and providing a good service to all because you will receive the same treatment from the Lord. Employers are instructed to treat their employees in the same manner because their supervisor is the Lord.

Complete Day 3 – Workbook Activity (optional)

DAY FOUR

Put on the Full Armor
Ephesians 6:10 – 13

First, be strong in the Lord and the power of His might. Then, put on the full armor of God to stand firmly against the schemes of the devil. The strength and power of the Lord come from knowing that Jesus is above all and reigns over all the spiritual enemies. *"For our struggle is not against flesh and blood, but against the rulers, against the authorities, against the powers of this dark world and against the spiritual forces of evil in the heavenly realms."*

Satan's main goal is to kill, steal, and destroy our relationship with God and keep us from bearing fruit. However, with God's strength, might, and spiritual armor of protection, Christians can courageously stand guard against the attacks of the spiritual enemies and be a conqueror in Christ.

The Spiritual Weapons
Ephesians 6:14 – 17

Paul said get prepared and be ready to stand firm in Jesus Christ against the enemy by girding the waist with the belt of truth, putting on the breastplate of righteousness, and protecting the feet with the gospel of peace. Also, take up the shield of faith to extinguish all the flaming arrows of the evil one. Put on the helmet of salvation and grasp the sword of the Spirit, which is the Word of God.

Power of Prayer
Ephesians 6:18 – 24

"And pray in the Spirit on all occasions with all kinds of prayers and requests. With this in mind, be alert and always keep on praying for all the Lord's people."

Paul asked the Ephesians to pray for him to have the right words and the holy boldness to share with others the mystery of the gospel for the sake of Christ. Paul sends his letter of encouragement by way of Tychicus, a faithful minister in the Lord, to share with the Ephesians on how and what he is doing. Paul ends his letter with *"Grace to all who love our Lord Jesus Christ with an undying love."*

Complete Day 4 – Workbook Activity (optional)

DAY FIVE
Reflection

<u>The Mighty Armor of God</u>

*"Then Jesus said to those Jews who believed Him, "If you **abide in My word**, you are My disciples indeed. And you shall know the **truth**, and the truth shall make you free" (John 8:31 – 32, NKJV).*

Paul was imprisoned in Rome for two years in a house that he rented. He was free to move about the house and receive visitors while the Roman soldiers guarded him during the day. (Acts 28:30 – 31). However, he was shackled to a Roman soldier at night while he slept to ensure that he would not escape before his trial. Paul must have spent a lot of time looking at the soldiers and their armor. Some Bible scholars believe that Paul used the imagery of a Roman soldier to describe the spiritual weapons and the Armor of God.

Paul said that the Armor is created by the grace of God to protect us from the schemes of the devil and his enemies. It is also designed to strengthen our faith and prepare us for our purpose, which is to bear fruit for the Lord. The spiritual weapons that God provides allow us to stand guard, stand firm, and steadfast in His truth against the evil one. We can stand strong and persevere against the temptations of sin through the truth found in the Word of God and the power of prayer. In Ephesians, Paul shares how to use God's spiritual weapons to battle and defeat Satan.

We receive the **Breastplate of Righteousness** through our faith in Jesus Christ. God's gift of grace and His righteousness protect our **heart** from the enemy when he tries to throw accusations of guilt and shame against us. The **Helmet of Salvation** protects the **mind** from listening to Satan's lies of discouragement and doubt. We have the hope and assurance of our salvation to overcome temptations and not surrender to Satan's lies in knowing that Christ has already won the war for us. We take up the **Shield of Faith** to extinguish Satan's fiery arrows of deceit and conquer feelings of pride, fear, anxiety, and depression.

The **Gospel of Peace** prepares our **soul** and moves our feet to be ready to answer those who ask us about our faith. When given the opportunity to share the gospel, we do so with gentleness, humility, and out of reverence for God. We stand on the promises of God to give us the **strength** to defeat Satan by using the **Belt of Truth and the Sword of the Spirit.** The **Belt** secures the waist with biblical beliefs, principles, and promises while the **Sword** (Word of God) helps us stand firm on the truth and the power of prayer.

⁹Adapted from, https://enduringword.com/bible-commentary/ephesians-6/

Complete Day 5 – Workbook Activity (optional)

Week 4

WITH ALL MY STRENGTH

The Thorn in my Flesh – Arrogance

I had just completed one year of teaching at my new school. I did not make an effort to build friendships or become involved in the church community where I lived because I knew it would be short-lived. I planned to work and live in this small town for two years until I received my masters and then move on.

I was not concerned with asking God for His advice, will, or plan for my life. I was in the driver's seat and completely turned a deaf ear to God's truth and wisdom. I did what I wanted, I had the boyfriend (Steve) that I wanted, and I continued to drink whenever and whatever I wanted. The thorn of arrogance pierced deeply into my soul as I convinced myself that I was in charge of my life, my happiness, and my outcomes.

During the summer, I noticed that my stomach was protruding profusely. I had gained several pounds from not exercising and from my poor eating habits. I was scheduled to go on vacation in July with the girlfriends that I worked with at my former school. I told my friends about my weight gain and while on the beach in a bikini they noticed, too.

One of my friends said that I looked six months pregnant.

...*God* will strengthen you with his own *great power* so that you will not give up when troubles come, but you will **be patient.**

Colossians 1:11 (NCV)

I assured her that I was not. I blew off her comment by saying it was just happy fat. She fussed at me and said that I better go to the doctor and have it checked out as soon as we got home. I was not concerned about my belly until my friend made a big deal about it. I just thought since my mother has a short-waist and gains all of her weight in her stomach then I must have the same genes, too.

I took my friends advice and made a doctor's appointment when I returned from my vacation. I saw a female doctor in the town where I lived. The teachers that I worked with said that she was a very "progressive" doctor. She would be determined to find out what was wrong with my stomach. On the day of my doctor's visit, she took one look at me and said that I had fluid in my abdomen. She rushed me into another room and before I knew it, stuck a long, huge syringe into my stomach and began draining a bloody fluid.

She said, "Let's get this fluid off and stomach down." The vain side of me said, "Yes, let's do it!" She drained 2 liters of fluid off of my stomach. Yes, imagine a 2-liter soda bottle that is how much she drained. My stomach was semi-flat again, I was pleased with the results, and told her, "Thank you, way to go, and see ya!" She said, "Not so fast. We need to have this fluid sent to the lab and tested for cancer." WHAT? Cancer, seriously?

That evening I told my parents about my doctor's visit. My mom's younger sister, who is a nurse, called to talk to me. I told her what happened and she said the doctor had no right to drain that much fluid off of me without running some tests first. Even if she did run the tests, an OBGYN should not have taken those types of aggressive measures.

Let's just say she scared and convinced me enough to make an appointment with a gastroenterologist. The gastro doctor did a CAT scan on me and said that I had a cyst or tumor the size of a grapefruit growing out of the left side of my ovary. He referred me to a female surgeon at a cancer clinic in a metropolitan area.

My parents were extremely concerned about the test results. It was the first time that I had seen my dad worried about me. My dad and I have had somewhat of an estranged relationship. Our relationship is better now than it has ever been, but it took years of arguments and disagreements to get there.

While growing up, I always had an arrogant and rebellious nature. When reprimanded as a child, I would comply, agree, and listen to my dad's advice, but ultimately, I did what I wanted. Seeing my dad withdraw and become worried about me was a shock. I didn't know how much he loved me until I observed his behavior for the two weeks we waited for the lab results.

When my lab results from the "progressive doctor" had come in, she said that I did not have cancer. I told her that the gastro doctor found a cyst and had already referred me to a surgeon. She said, "But you don't have cancer. All you need is laparoscopic surgery to remove the cyst. I can do that for you at the hospital here in town." It sounded ideal to me, but my mom and aunt convinced me to use the surgeon.

After surgery, I moved in with my parents to recuperate for six weeks while a substitute teacher took my place at work. I wish I could say this was a wake-up call or turning point for me, but it wasn't. I continued to overindulge and do whatever I wanted to reinforce my arrogance.

While recuperating, the surgeon prescribed birth control pills to help me deal with the hormonal changes. I did not fill the prescription. I blamed the birth control pills for putting me in this situation. I thought the extra estrogen from the birth control pills caused the cyst.

I'm not sure if there was a correlation or not, but after my surgery when my left ovary ovulated I had extreme pain on my left side during my menstrual cycle. Also, I was extremely hormonal, aka moody, before and or after my period. The moodiness seemed to occur every other month. I didn't want to take medication or even see a doctor about my symptoms due to the stigma attached to being emotionally unstable. I suffered in silence with my emotions and self-medicated with alcohol for years before asking for help.

Eventually, my symptoms led me to ask an OBGYN for advice. The doctor prescribed Sarafem (Prozac) for me to take a few days before and during my periods. This remedy was a temporary fix. It was many years later when I realized that I needed to take medication every day to subside my hormonal symptoms. The medicine is not perfect, but it does help me manage my moodiness, irritability, and sadness a few days before, during, and right after my menstrual cycle.

I am aware that Satan uses this weakness against me. If I am not careful, during the hormonal times, I am more susceptible to the temptations of alcohol to help balance my moodiness, irritability, and or restlessness. I have to be intentional in my thinking and behaviors in submitting to God and asking the Holy Spirit to help me resist these temptations.

I cognitively put on the Helmet of Salvation to focus my thoughts on the things above and protect my mind from giving into the evil one. Through abiding in Jesus, I fasten the Breastplate of Righteousness over my chest to guard my heart against having a negative attitude.

My flesh is very fragile during menstruation. Therefore, I boldly ask the Holy Spirit for the strength to resist Satan's lies and schemes by securing my waist with the Belt of Truth and the Sword of the Spirit. Then, I take up the Shield of Faith and the power of prayer to conquer feelings of doubt, anxiety, and depression.

Week 4 – The Promises of God
Paul's Letter to the Colossians 1 – 4

Overview

Paul received visitors while under house arrest in Rome. One was a fellow minister from Colossae named Epaphras. He reported that false teachings and the Colossian heresy were spreading throughout the tri-city area. The heresy was a combination of pagan and Jewish practices involving four elements: philosophies of men, Judaism ceremonies, angel worship, and abstinence (laws about what to eat or drink).

Paul wrote a letter to the Colossian Christians encouraging them to protect their minds from returning to idol worship and to focus on Christ, instead. Paul prayed for them to have the wisdom, spiritual understanding, and discernment to do God's will. He prayed that their spiritual walk would be worthy, pleasing, and fruitful as they grew in the knowledge and wisdom of God. He prayed for them to find strength, patience, and joy in their longsuffering, as he did, through the glorious power of the Lord Jesus Christ.

Focus on the Things Above

It was important to Paul for the Colossians to protect their minds from the false teachings and heresies in the land. The image below is an illustration of Paul's advice to them on how to protect their minds from sin.

Paul's first concern was that they **pray** to have the **faith**, understanding, and wisdom to do God's will. The fulfillment of God's will would require them to **persevere** in the **truth** and revelations of the gospel by continuing to walk in faith.

He asked that they **bind their hearts** together in **love** with other believers to strengthen, encourage, and unite their faith. This bond would help them rebuke false teachings and protect their minds from evil.

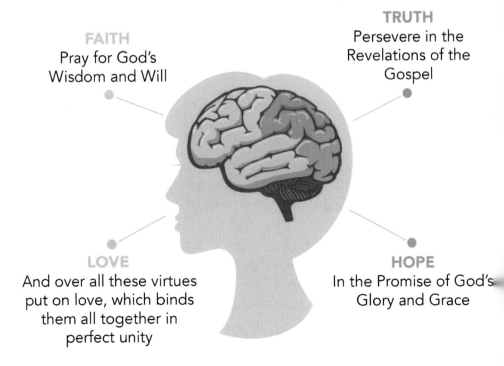

FAITH
Pray for God's
Wisdom and Will

TRUTH
Persevere in the
Revelations of the
Gospel

LOVE
And over all these virtues
put on love, which binds
them all together in
perfect unity

HOPE
In the Promise of God's
Glory and Grace

Paul said, to have **hope** in the **promises** of God. Since they will know us by our deeds, put to death the deeds of the flesh and focus our mind on the **hope of God's glory and grace** in a spirit of humility and gratitude.

DAY ONE

To Know Jesus and what He expects
Colossians 1:1 – 8

Epaphras was a minister from Colossae and responsible for sharing the gospel in the tri-city area of Colossae, Hierapolis, and Laodicea. He went to visit Paul in Rome to talk to him about the false teachings that were spreading throughout the land.

Although Paul probably never traveled to or preached in Colossae, he was thankful for the strong faith, hope and love they had for Jesus, their fellow saints, and the gospel. Out of Christian concern, Paul wrote to the Colossians on how to protect their minds from false teachings and heresies. He explained that the answer is to know and understand who Jesus is and what He expects of them.

How to please God and have a Worthy Walk
Colossians 1:9 – 14

Paul prayed the Colossians would be filled with the knowledge of God's will in all spiritual wisdom and understanding. He asked God to strengthen them to live and walk in the will and wisdom of the Lord. In doing so, they would be fruitful in every good work and given the desire to know God.

Paul said being fruitful and growing in knowledge is how to please God and have a walk that is worthy of Him, doing so with endurance, patience, and joy. Paul knew the opposite of this would bring foolishness, unwise decisions, and ultimately self-destruction.

He explained there are four ways to protect and focus the mind on the knowledge and wisdom of God.

Wisdom #1: Know the Son of God
Colossians 1:15 – 20

Jesus is the image of God, the firstborn over all creation, and all things were created by Him, through Him, and for Him to make His glory known. Therefore, ALL things were created to serve and magnify the glory of the Savior. He is the source of the church and the divine firstborn from the dead. *"For God was pleased to have all his fullness dwell in him."*

In Christ alone, there is hope, grace, redemption, the forgiveness of sins, and salvation because He took our place and the judgment of our sins on the cross. We experience reconciliation and peace with God through Jesus Christ, in order, to be presented holy and blameless before Him.

Wisdom #2: The Hope found in the Gospel
Colossians 1:21 – 23

Paul told the Colossians, *"Once you were alienated from God and were enemies in your minds because of your evil behavior. But now he has reconciled you by Christ's physical body through death to present you holy in his sight, without blemish and free from accusation— if you continue in your faith, established and firm, and do not move from the hope held out in the gospel."*

Paul said you must continue to believe this truth, stand firm in faith, and do not forsake the hope found in the gospel. The gospel provides the knowledge of the Son of God and what He did for them. Paul knew his mission was to spread the good news of the gospel because God uses the power and truth of the gospel to save and reconcile His people to Him.

Wisdom #3: Hope in the Glory of God
Colossians 1:24 – 25

Paul rejoiced in his sufferings for their sake so that the gospel and the hope of glory would be made real and known to them. Paul considered it a privilege to suffer for the body of Christ. He demonstrated Christ's sufferings to others because Christ suffered to save and redeem him. Paul's sufferings for Christ gave him the joy of his salvation and the hope of abiding in the glory of God for eternity.

Wisdom #4: Be Fruitful in every Good Work
Colossians 1:26 – 29

Paul accepted and followed God's will for his ministry to spread the gospel of grace. He revealed how salvation through faith in Jesus is available to all the nations, both the Jews and Gentiles. This mystery, which was kept hidden from the past generations, was now being proclaimed under the new covenant promise. God justifies the Jews and Gentiles for their belief and faith in Jesus Christ. For this was Paul's calling and struggle, to be fruitful in every good work and present everyone fully mature in Christ.

Complete Day 1 – Workbook Activity (optional)

DAY TWO

Some of the false teachers in Colossae advocated that salvation could only be understood by the intellectually, select few who were "called" to be spiritual. But, Paul's calling came directly from God to spread the good news of the gospel and reveal to all the nations the truth about Christ.

Paul prayed the Colossians would bind their hearts together in **love** with other believers to strengthen their **faith and hope in God's truth**.

And this is the secret:
Christ lives in you.
This gives you assurance of
sharing his glory.

Colossians 1:27 (NLT)

This accountability would help them resist the temptations of sin and protect their minds from false teachings.

<u>Do not be deceived by False Teachings</u>
Colossians 2:1 – 7

Paul struggled inwardly for the Colossians and those in Laodicea. The philosophies being taught appeared to be highly intelligent, making it appealing and desirable, rather than sinful. He encouraged them to unite and stand strong in love and the full assurance of their salvation.

Paul explained that the treasures of wisdom, knowledge, and salvation are not found in the philosophies of these false teachings, but in Christ alone. Paul said even though he was not physically with them, he was with them in spirit because of their good order and steadfastness in the faith. Paul encouraged them again to **grow in Christ**, to be **rooted and built up** in Him, **grounded** in the faith as they were trained, and to do these things with a thankful spirit.

Colossians 2:8 – 10

The false teachers were very persuasive in their hidden agenda that wisdom and knowledge are attainable without a belief in Jesus. Paul completely dispelled these false teachings by saying that only in Christ dwells the fullness of God and not in some mystical or angelic being.

All the fullness of the Godhead (God's divine nature) is in Jesus's body, which is why we are complete in Him, the deity of Christ. The fullness of the Father's nature is also in the Son. By God's grace, we are reconciled to Him through Jesus and can have a love relationship with Him. Furthermore, God is above all and overall spiritual principalities and false powers.

<u>Spiritually Circumcised</u>
Colossians 2:11 – 17

Most of the Colossian Christians were Gentiles and not physically circumcised. The false teachers said they needed to be circumcised in order to be "holy," based on their religious laws and sanctification principles. Paul insisted that this physical act was not necessary for them to glorify God.

They were already spiritually circumcised by putting away the sins of the flesh and being built up in Jesus through faith. Paul said, if you need to perform an act then perform the act of baptism. This act would demonstrate how the old self and its sins are dead and buried in Christ. But, the new self is made alive and resurrected through faith.

Paul proclaimed that they were once dead in their trespasses and flesh, but now they have been born again. God has forgiven them and wiped out the debt they owed by nailing it to the cross. Jesus conquered all of these false teachings, principalities, and mystical powers. "He made a public spectacle of them, triumphing over them by the cross." Therefore, do not let anyone judge you by abstaining from food or drink, or with regard to celebrating religious festivals or holy days.

Warnings against Spiritual Pride and Arrogance
Colossians 2:18 – 23

The false teachers took pride in their philosophies, ceremonies, abstinence, and worship of angelic beings. They were vain and arrogant about the secrets they kept and took pleasure in their false humility. Paul said this is not God's plan for the body of the church. The church grows when the body is committed and connected to Christ, and not to the laws or regulations about food or drink.

People perform the rules of legalism in man's strength, rather than, relying on God for His strength to deliver them from temptation and sin. Therefore, legalism has an appearance of wisdom, false humility, and self-discipline of the body, but it does not require faith, especially for your sanctification. Paul posed the question, "If by faith you died to the old self and rose with Christ a new, why do you continue to follow these deceitful laws?"

> *...our old self was crucified with Him...*
> *Romans 6:6*

Complete Day 2 – Workbook Activity (optional)

I have been crucified with Christ and I no longer live, but **Christ lives in me.**

Galatians 2:20 (NIV)

DAY THREE

On Things Above
Colossians 3:1 –13

Paul said, *"Since, then, you have been raised with Christ, set your hearts on things above, where Christ is, seated at the right hand of God. Set your minds on things above, not on earthly things. For you died, and your life is now hidden with Christ in God. When Christ, who is your life, appears, then you also will appear with him in glory."*

Therefore, think like Christ, behave like Christ, and seek to be with Him in glory. Since your identity is in Christ; put to death your old habits, such as fornication, uncleanness, evil desires, and covetousness, which is idolatry. Get rid of the (habitual) sins that lead to self-destruction, condemnation, and the wrath of God, as a result of disobedience, and walk in the truth.

Put on the new self, which is renewed in knowledge after the image of its creator, because Christ is all, and in all, whosoever believes. *"Therefore, as God's chosen people, holy and dearly loved, clothe yourselves with compassion, kindness, humility, gentleness, and patience. Bear with each other and forgive one another… as the Lord forgave you."*

Put on Love
Colossians 3:14 – 17

Paul said above all these things put on love and let the peace of Christ live in the hearts of all believers. Let the word of Christ dwell within you, learn from one another, apply Christ's example, and sing songs of praise. He said to do all these things in the name of Jesus by giving thanks to God the Father.

Christian Living
Colossians 3:18 – 25

Paul said a wife should submit to her husband as is fitting in the Lord. As a wife, I believe it is part of her Christian responsibility. The phrase has more to do with her attitude and motive for submitting rather than oppression.

I think if her heart and attitude are pure and right before God, she will have the willingness to respect and honor her husband as the head of the home. The husband, as the respected head of the household, should love his wife in an attitude of self-denial and a self-giving love.

Likewise, children should obey their father and mother for this is well pleasing to the Lord. When children show respect to their parents, they are also respecting God. Parents have the responsibility of not provoking their children to sin.

As Christians, putting on the new self also means to work for your employer with a sense of loyalty. And whatever you do, do it as if you are working for the Lord and not for men, knowing that your eternal reward is in heaven.

Complete Day 3 – Workbook Activity (optional)

DAY FOUR

<u>The Gift of Prayer</u>
Colossians 4:1 – 6

Paul asked the Colossians to pray diligently and with a grateful attitude that God would continue to prosper them. He asked them to pray that God would create opportunities for him and his fellow ministers to courageously preach the gospel.

Paul requested that the Colossians learn and understand biblical truths in answering questions from outsiders about Christianity. He said to talk and walk in the wisdom of Christ and to always respond with grace, seasoned carefully as with salt, so you will know how to answer each person.

Paul's Faithful Messengers

Colossians 4:7 – 14

Epaphras visited Paul and delivered the news to him about the Colossians, but Paul's letter would be sent back to Colossae through Tychicus and Onesimus, a former servant of Philemon. Paul wrote to the Colossians to update them on his activities and encourage them in their faithful walk with the Lord.

Paul mentioned three other ministers who are of Jewish descent and a comfort to him while he is in prison. Then, Paul references Epaphras, who he described as a servant of Christ laboring in prayer for the Colossians. Paul prayed that Epaphras would stand perfect and complete in the will of God, regardless of the false teachings that were in the land.

Paul sent the Colossian's greetings from Demas and the physician Luke, who was probably in Rome to deliver his writings on the Gospel of Luke and the Book of Acts. These close companions of Paul visited and supported him during his house arrest in Rome while awaiting his trial before Caesar.

Colossians 4:15 – 18

Paul asked the Colossians to greet their brethren in the neighboring cities at the house churches. If there was not a church building for congregates, people gathered in the homes of the church leaders. He specifically said to read his letter in the house churches at Laodicea and to tell Archippus to continue in his ministry, despite the false teachings. Lastly, Paul asked them to pray and remember his chains due to the uncertainty of his trial before Caesar's court. He ends the letter with *"Grace be with you"* as you continue in the fruitful works of God."

Complete Day 4 – Workbook Activity (optional)

DAY FIVE
Reflection

Having Hope in God's Glory and Grace

We become stronger in our hope for the future when we give God all the glory for His grace. Paul understood and lived out the gift of faith. He found joy, peace, and perseverance in his sufferings for Christ's sake. Paul could rejoice in his sufferings because he focused on the wisdom of his faith, the hope of the gospel, the truth of his salvation, and his love and desire for the Kingdom of heaven.

Paul knew that the things of this world and its desires would perish, but having hope in God's glory, grace, and revelations sustained him. He knew his time and sufferings on earth were temporary compared to his reward in heaven and spending eternity with God.

Paul said knowing the Word of God allows the mind to focus on God's promises by seeking His humility and the hope of His glory. The hope of His glory produces the fruit of love. This transforming love gives Christians the willingness to deny self, put others first, and suffer for the sake of Christ to demonstrate His love for the world. These acts of love are made possible through faith and the power of Jesus Christ.

Paul said we are all a part of the encompassing family of God, regardless of race, socioeconomic status, or culture. The new-self becomes renewed in wisdom by reading and studying the Word of God, worshipping with other believers, and daily prayer. Prayer is the rock-solid foundation that we build our relationship with Jesus upon.

Without prayer and faith, it is impossible to please God and to have a relationship with our Creator and Savior. For we cannot save ourselves, we are saved by His grace through faith, which is God's gift to us. The gift of prayer and faith give us the confidence to boldly go to the throne of God with the blessed assurance that all things work together for our good, despite the sufferings and hardships that we endure in this world.

Complete Day 5 – Workbook Activity (optional)

May you always be filled with the fruit of your *salvation*—the righteous character produced in your life by *Jesus Christ*—for this will bring much glory and *praise to God*.

Philippians 1:11 (NLT)

$\mathcal{W}eek$ 5

WITH ALL MY SOUL

The Thorn in My Soul – Dishonesty

When I first met Steve, I discovered that he worked the swing shift at a factory in his hometown. I did not even know how swing shift hours worked. He worked four days in a row and then was off for four days. The next shift he worked four nights in a row and then was off for four nights. It seemed like an exhausting schedule, and it was.

His home was a two-hour drive from the University town where I lived. The first weekend that he was not working he wanted me to meet his four-year-old son who lived with him. I agreed and drove on a Friday after work to his house to meet his son. When I arrived, to my surprise, I learned that Steve's mom also lived with him. She took care of the child while Steve worked the swing shift hours.

I was apprehensive about meeting little Steve. I had never considered dating a guy who had a child before. I walked in and was immediately under the spell of this mini version of Steve. He was precious and had the cutest personality. He was very comfortable around me which made it easy for me to show him love and kindness.

The only thing I looked forward to all week was driving every weekend to be with Steve. I consciously decided that

93

I would be a good girlfriend. I would not play games or act hard to get. I would be loving and considerate toward Steve. I was never confrontational, just agreeable to keep from getting hurt again.

I went along to get along and did this for two years while we were in a long-distance relationship. At the time, I didn't realize this type of passive behavior was dishonest. I was dishonest with myself and Steve by hiding my true nature and not voicing my opinions or concerns.

After graduating with my master's degree, I moved in with my parents to be closer to Steve. I was now twenty minutes from Steve, instead of two hours. I landed a good local job and the driving every weekend had come to an end. So, I thought.

Steve's ex-wife and husband lived about a three-hour drive from Steve. Every Friday after work, I drove little Steve an hour and a half, halfway, to meet his stepdad so he could spend the weekend with his mom and half-brother. This driving arrangement lasted for about a year and a half.

Steve's mother accepted a new job and relocated an hour away from him. Steve began to panic. His ex-wife took him to court for custody of their child. When the judge asked Steve how he was going to care for his son, now that his mother was leaving the area, Steve's quick response was that he was engaged and planned to have his new wife help him. This was the first time Steve had ever mentioned the word engaged or wife to me.

Later, he asked me what I thought about us getting married. I said, "Are you asking me to marry you so you can get custody of your son?" He said, no that he was asking because he really did want to marry me. I told him that I was confused and just didn't know. I needed to speak to my parents about it, and so I did.

My mom was thrilled and said how much she loved Steve and his son. My dad, on the other hand, was not buying it. He said, "You do realize that you will always be third in Steve's life." I asked my dad, "What do you mean?" He said, "Steve's job ranks; first, his son is second, and you come in third. If you can accept that, then marry Steve." I thought, wow, what a slap in the face. I said, "Why are you just now saying this to me after three and a half years of dating Steve?" He said, "I thought you would figure it out for yourself by now, but obviously, not."

His words of truth crushed my already wounded spirit. To protect my hurt, I lied to myself by saying that life would be okay with Steve. I would prove my dad wrong. I refused to ask or even listen to God and allow the Holy Spirit to breathe truth and hope into my situation. I did what I wanted. I did not pursue God's will. I persevered in my own strength.

We became engaged. A few weeks later, Steve lost custody of his son. I convinced myself that since I invested so much time in my relationship with Steve and his son that I should marry him. I was in my late twenties. All of my sorority friends were already married and had kids. It just seemed like the next step in life. We were married six months later.

Once again, I went along to get along while resentment and bitterness settled into my *heart*, anger and unforgiveness consumed my *thoughts*, alcohol soothed my *flesh*, and lying to myself had overtaken my *soul*. Based on the lack of communication and commitment on my part, I decided to divorce Steve.

I did repent and ask for God's forgiveness. It took me a long time to realize that there is no condemnation for those who are in Christ. Jesus forgave me when he died on the cross. I just needed to live out this truth.

I learned that life is not about what I can do for God, but what He has already done for me. As I ask Jesus to help me resist daily temptations, surrender my will, and walk in the Spirit, I praise Him for the glorious grace that He has poured out on me, Bridget, who belongs to His dear Son (Ephesians 1:6, NLT).

Week 5 – The Glory of God
Paul's Letter to the Philippians 1 – 4

Overview

Although Paul was under house arrest in Rome, his missionary goal was always to further the gospel and Kingdom of God. He greatly loved the Philippians for their prayers and support of him during these trying times. Paul's example and sufferings for Christ gave the Philippians the confidence and boldness they needed to persist and spread the gospel while they prayed and waited for Paul's return.

Paul's faith in God's grace and the Philippians' prayers sustained him. The Spirit of God was Paul's source of strength and joy. He trusted that, despite his trials, he would remain in the will of God, the joy of the Lord, and continue to bear much fruit for Him.

DAY ONE

Paul sends greetings to the Christians at Philippi
Philippians 1:1 – 8

During Paul's second missionary journey, he started the first church in Europe at Philippi. Paul was grateful to the Philippians for their prayers and financial support of his ministry from day one until even now while in prison.

Paul said, *"Being confident of this, that he who began a good work in you will carry it on to completion until the day of Christ Jesus."* Paul explained how they were both partakers in God's grace by his imprisonment and in the spreading of the gospel. He was thankful and joyful for their prayers and commitment to spreading the gospel even in his absence.

Paul's prayer for the Philippians
Philippians 1:9 – 11

Paul greatly loved the Philippians. They loved him, too. He prayed their love would abound even more in knowledge and discernment. He prayed they would only approve those things that are excellent, pure, and blameless before Christ.

He asked God to make them both sincere and without any offense or wrongdoings toward others. Paul said this occurred from being filled with the fruit of righteousness as they abide in Jesus Christ. The result was bearing fruit and bringing glory and praise to God.

Furtherance of the Gospel
Philippians 1:12 – 14

Paul wanted to encourage the Philippians not to lose heart and to assure them that God had a purpose for his imprisonment and possible execution. The furtherance of the gospel was still taking place even while Paul was in prison.

Paul used this time to write letters to the Colossians, Ephesians, and Philippians, as well as, witness to and convert the palace guards and many others. Paul's Christian example and imprisonment gave other missionaries the courage and confidence to boldly preach the gospel without fear and bring glory to the Lord.

Preach from Good Will
Philippians 1:15 – 18

Paul realized that some were motivated to preach the gospel out of selfish ambition, self-promotion, and competition, instead of good will. Those competing with Paul in the ministry were glad he was in prison because in their mind he was no longer a threat.

Paul knew these ministers had wrong motives because their focus was on having a successful image, rather than serving with a sincere heart. Either way, he rejoiced that the truth of the gospel was being preached no matter the motivation.

Christ Magnified
Philippians 1:19 – 26

Paul believed through the Philippians' constant prayers that he was supplied with the Spirit of Christ to help meet and sustain his needs and deliver him from prison. Paul was not ashamed of his trials because he knew that he was in the will of God and his purpose was to bear fruit.

Paul placed all of his hopeful trust in the promises of God, whether in life or death, by his example Christ would be glorified. For Paul, to live for the sake of spreading the gospel of Christ was gain and to die for Christ and to be with Him in glory was the ultimate reward.

Nevertheless, Paul had faith that the Romans would not execute him. Eventually, he would be reunited with the Philippians to share in their progress, unity, and joyfulness in Christ.

Philippians 1:27 – 30

Paul told the Philippians that no matter what happened to him, whether he lives or dies for the sake of Christ, to always conduct yourself in a manner that is worthy of the gospel. Therefore, in his presence or absence, stand firm and strive together in one Spirit for the faith of the gospel.

Paul said do not be frightened by spiritual enemies or by those who oppose you because this is proof that they will soon perish, but God will save you. God is in control of your present trials.

He allows trials and suffering for His sake, for you to be used by God as a vessel to further His kingdom. *"For it has been granted to you on behalf of Christ not only to believe in him, but also to suffer for him, since you are going through the same struggle you saw I had, and now hear that I still have."*

Complete Day 1 – Workbook Activity (optional)

Share the Gospel of Truth	Believe in "To live is Christ, to die is gain."	Steadfast Unity and Joyfulness in Christ
Christ's Death, Resurrection, & Second Coming	Put Hopeful Trust & Faith in the Promises of God	Magnifies & Glorifies the Lord

DAY TWO

Paul's Invitation
Philippians 2:1 – 4

Paul asked the Philippians four rhetorical questions about their unity and joyfulness in Christ. He said if you have encouragement in Christ, the comfort of His love, fellowship in the Spirit, the affection and the mercy of God—then it is your responsibility to share the gospel of truth with unbelievers. Paul asked them to fulfill the joy of unity by standing in agreement, having the same love for one another, and being of one mind.

Then, Paul explained how to achieve the joy of unity that leads to magnifying and glorifying the Lord. He said, "*Do nothing out of selfish ambition or vain conceit. Rather, in humility value others above yourselves, not looking to your own interests but each of you to the interests of the others.*"

The Mind of Christ
Philippians 2:5 – 11

Paul said to choose the mindset of Christ, who being in the form of God, humbled Himself in love and obedience to God, even to the point of death on a cross for the salvation of humankind. While on earth, Jesus did not give up His deity, any of His characteristics, or His equality with God, instead he added to His deity by taking on the form of a servant and coming in the real likeness of man. *"Therefore, God exalted Him to the highest place and gave Him the name that is above every name, that at the name of Jesus every knee should bow, in heaven and on earth and under the earth, and every tongue acknowledge that Jesus Christ is Lord, to the glory of God the Father."*

Work Out Your Salvation
Philippians 2:12 – 18

Paul encouraged the Philippians to "work out" their salvation with fear and trembling, *"for it is God who works in you to will and to act in order to fulfill His good purpose."* Therefore, do not resent God for any sufferings or persecutions, do not dispute with or harm one another, instead be accountable to one another, true followers of God, put others' interests before your own, and shine among others like stars in the sky.

Paul encouraged them to hold steadfast to the Word of God, which is life, so they can be proud and rejoice in their fruitful works on the day of Christ's return. Paul said for these same reasons rejoice with me now in either life or death, (in case his trial ends in martyrdom), because their commitment and trust in God brings glory to the Lord. *"But even if I am being poured out like a drink offering on the sacrifice and service coming from your faith, I am glad and rejoice with all of you. So you too should be glad and rejoice with me."*

Timothy and Epaphroditus
Philippians 2:19 – 30

Paul told the Philippians that Timothy, who sincerely cares for them, would check on them after the trial. He said they could trust Timothy, because even as a child, Timothy with his father served with Paul in the gospel. Paul believed the Lord would send him to Philippi when the trial was over. Paul sent his letter to the Philippians by way of

Epaphroditus, who was from Philippi.

While Epaphroditus was traveling to Rome, to provide financial support and minister to Paul, he became very sick to the point of death. Paul was thankful that God had mercy on Epaphroditus and he eventually became well. Paul was also thankful that Epaphroditus did not die for it would be sorrowful for Paul to lose a fellow brother, but even more so, to lose him for traveling to Rome to be with him. Paul asked the Philippians to receive Epaphroditus for the selfless work he had done and to rejoice upon his return.

Complete Day 2 – Workbook Activity (optional)

DAY THREE

Rejoice in the Lord
Philippians 3:1 – 4

Paul told the Philippians to rejoice because the Lord is working all things together for their good. Paul felt a great need to warn and keep them safe from the practice of legalism. He said to be aware of the dogs, those of the legal persuasion because these evil workers create drama and strife. He told them to be cautious of the legalists who insist that Gentiles must first become Jews (circumcised) in order to become a Christian and fulfill the Law of Moses.

The Jewish legalists believed circumcision made them blameless before God. But, Paul said, *"For it is we who are the circumcision, we who serve God by His Spirit, who boast in Christ Jesus, and who put no confidence in the flesh."* Therefore, Paul and his brethren knew that circumcision and law-keeping did not justify them before God. Justification only comes through faith in Jesus Christ.

<u>Works of the Flesh</u>
Philippians 3:5 – 11

Paul, a Jewish descendant and well educated in Judaism law, knew that he was more qualified than any legalist when it came to having confidence in the works of the flesh and law-keeping. Paul said if anyone could boast and defend himself by the rules of the Law it would be him.

Paul even provided the evidence. He was circumcised on the eighth day after he was born, a descendant of Abraham, Isaac, and Jacob, part of the same covenant God had with them, and from the tribe of Benjamin, which is the same lineage as Saul, Israel's first king. Paul was raised an elite Hebrew by his parents and a Pharisee, known for their strict devotion and obedience to the Law. Regarding zeal for the Law, Paul actively persecuted the church and achieved a status of righteousness and blamelessness among the Jewish legalists in his effort to please God by the works of the flesh.

Paul said that all of these earthly things are rubbish and considered a loss compared to the eternal rewards and glory of Christ. Paul said, *"But whatever were gains to me I now consider loss for the sake of Christ."* Paul humbly suffered the loss of his status in legalism to gain wisdom, knowledge, and a personal relationship with Christ.

Paul explained that he no longer trusts in the Law or his righteousness, but instead puts his confidence and faith in the righteousness of Christ. Paul had a strong desire to know Jesus, to grow in the power of His resurrection, and to fellowship in His sufferings, even if this meant execution by the Romans. He did not fear the loss of death because he considered being with Jesus in heaven and the resurrection of his earthly body as the ultimate reward.

<u>Press On</u>
Philippians 3:12 – 16

Paul said, *"Not that I have already obtained all this, or have already arrived at my goal, but I press on to take hold of that for which Christ Jesus took hold of me."* He said there is no looking back only striving forward to what lies ahead. *"I press on toward the goal to win the prize for which God has called me heavenward in Christ Jesus."*

Paul believed the call itself, being an instrument of righteousness for the Lord to do His work and further His kingdom, was the prize. He said Jesus began a good work in him. He was determined to see Jesus's work completed in and through him by bearing much fruit.

Paul said, as mature Christians, we must embrace the same mindset as Jesus, stay in unity, and apply these same principles when in opposition with one another. If you think otherwise, pray and ask the Lord to reveal the truth to you.

Seek Good Examples of the Walk
Philippians 3:17 – 21

Paul encouraged the Philippians to imitate his example as he imitates Christ. He said to find mentors in Philippi, who are already walking in the faith, for guidance. For many claim the walk, but they set their minds on earthly things and are enemies of the cross in how they disrespect biblical truths. They repeatedly indulge in the sensual pleasures of the mind, body, and soul. They glorify in the very acts that they should be ashamed of committing. Paul said this lifestyle leads to a destructive end.

Paul reminded the Philippians that they are citizens of heaven and to conduct themselves accordingly. *"But, our citizenship is in heaven. And we eagerly await a Savior from there, the Lord Jesus Christ, who, by the power that enables him to bring everything under his control, will transform our lowly bodies so that they will be like his glorious body."*

Complete Day 3 – Workbook Activity (optional)

DAY FOUR

The God of Peace and Strength
Philippians 4:1 – 9

Paul said to stand firm in the Lord, my beloved brethren, whom I long for, my joy and my crown. Help the two women, Euodia and Syntyche, who labored with me in the gospel, to reconcile their quarrels and have one mindset in the Lord, as well as Clement and the rest of my fellow workers. Despite these circumstances, *"Rejoice in the Lord always. I will say it again: Rejoice!"*

Paul said let your gentleness be shown to everyone because God is in control. *"Do not be anxious about anything, but in every situation, by prayer and petition, with thanksgiving, present your requests to God. And the peace of God, which transcends all understanding, will guard your hearts and your minds in Christ Jesus."*

Paul encouraged them to focus their mind on all things that are true, noble, just, pure, lovely, of good report, virtuous, praiseworthy, and to meditate on these things. Paul said to practice the things that you heard and saw me do. *"And the God of peace will be with you."*

To God be the Glory
Philippians 4:10 – 18

Paul thanked the Philippians for sending him financial support, by way of Epaphroditus, when they could afford to do so. Through his sufferings, he learned how to be humble. He also knew what it was like to have plenty. Paul recognized, no matter the circumstance, how to be content. *"I can do all this through Him who gives me strength."*

He told the Philippians they had done well, been a cheerful giver, and supported the cause. They supported him from the very start of his missionary work when no other church would. Even in

Forgetting what is behind, and straining toward what is *ahead*, I press on toward the goal to win the prize for which God has *called me heavenward* in Christ Jesus.

Philippians 3:13-14 (NIV)

Thessalonica, they sent aid to him twice. Paul did not take their gifts and generosity for granted because it helped him bear fruit for the Lord. The financial and personal support they gave blessed him like *"a fragrant offering, an acceptable sacrifice, pleasing to God."*

Philippians 4:19 – 23

Paul told them for their selfless and sacrificial giving, the Lord will supply what they need. There is no lack of supply according to the riches and glory in Christ Jesus. Paul said, in a spirit of thankfulness, may God be glorified forever and ever.

Paul reminded the Philippians to greet every Christian in Christ Jesus. He said my brethren, who are with me in Rome, send greetings to you all, especially the converted Christians from Caesar's household. Even in prison, Paul shared the gospel with Caesar's servants, guards, family members, and anyone he had an opportunity to witness to for Christ.

Complete Day 4 – Workbook Activity (optional)

DAY FIVE
Reflection

<u>Summary</u>

*"I pray that out of His glorious riches He may **strengthen** you with **power through His Spirit** in your inner being, so that Christ may dwell in your **hearts through faith**. And I pray that you, being **rooted and grounded in love**, may have power, together with all the Lord's holy people, **to grasp how wide and long and high and deep is the love of Christ**, and to know this **love** that surpasses knowledge—that you may be filled to the measure of all the **fullness of God**" (Ephesians 3:16 – 19).*

For me, this passage of Scripture is a real test of our faith, hope, and trust in Jesus. The only way to build a relationship with Jesus and experience the abundant life is to abide in Him, the true vine. Paul said, "I press on to take hold of that for which Christ Jesus took hold of me" (Philippians 3:12).

I want to encourage you to take root and hold of the Fruit of the Spirit, abide in Jesus by faith, grow and transform daily in the nourishment of His love, and fully prosper in His abundance.

"So then, just as you received Christ Jesus as Lord, continue to live your lives in him, rooted and built up in him, strengthened in the faith as you were taught, and overflowing with thankfulness" (Colossians 2:6 – 7).

By the grace of God, through Jesus Christ our Lord, we are set free from our habitual sins, the thorns of the old self. Paul said "to put off your old self, which is being corrupted by its deceitful desires; to be made new in the attitude of your minds; and to put on the new self, created to be like God in true righteousness and holiness" (Ephesians 4:22 – 24).

Jesus will give you the strength to put on the new self, but you must do your part. Pray with gratitude, live, serve, and bear fruit by practicing spirit-filled habits. It is not easy. When you cast your thorns or cares upon Him, Jesus releases you from carrying these burdens alone. By having hope and faith in all situations, this makes the yoke easy and gives rest and peace to your soul as you pursue the heart of Christ with a spirit of humility.

To pursue the heart of Christ is to abide in Him and follow His example. Where do we find His examples for daily living? We find it in the Word of God, the Sword of the Spirit. The Holy Spirit will help you follow Jesus's example, but once again, you must seek, ask, and pray for it. How do we present our requests to God?

"Do not be anxious about anything, but in every situation, by **prayer and petition,** with **thanksgiving,** present your requests to God. And the peace of God, which transcends all understanding, will guard your **hearts** and your **minds** in Christ Jesus" (Philippians 4:6-7).

"**Set your minds on things that are above, not on things that**

Abide in the True Vine

Ephesians
4:22-24

Philippians
4:6-7

Colossians
2:6-7

Ephesians
6:13-17

Philippians
3:12

Colossians
3:2-4

Ephesians
3:16-19

are on earth. For you have died, and your life is now hidden with Christ in God" (Colossians 3:2 – 3, ESV). You set your mind on things above by meditating on His Word, through prayer, praise music, Bible study, attending church, and surrounding yourself with people who worship God in the Spirit and truth.

"For our struggle is not against flesh and blood, but against the rulers, against the authorities, against the powers of this dark world and against the spiritual forces of evil in the heavenly realms" (Ephesians 6:12).

"Therefore, put on the full armor of God, so that when the day of evil comes, you may be able to stand your ground, and after you have done everything, to stand. Stand firm then, with the belt of truth buckled around your waist, with the breastplate of righteousness in place, and with your feet fitted with the readiness that comes from the gospel of peace. In addition to all this, take up the shield of faith, with which you can extinguish all the flaming arrows of the evil one. Take the helmet of salvation and the sword of the Spirit, which is the word of God" (Ephesians 6:13 – 17).

The only way to stand your ground against the schemes of the devil is to put on the full Armor of God every single day. Do not concern yourself with earthly desires or trials. Worrying about your trials or struggle is not going to change your situation one bit, but faith and prayer can change things for your good and His glory. Therefore, cast your cares, thorns, and burdens upon Him, and He will give you the resurrection power to conquer all things through Jesus Christ, who gives you the strength.

Complete Day 5 – Workbook Activity (optional)

APPENDIX
READER'S GUIDE

Appendix: Reader's Guide

The section on *God's Covenants* includes terms and background information needed for this study, such as the Covenant promises and Israel's Law-keeping to achieve justification.

The *Christian Movement* section introduces *The Day of Pentecost*, *The Story of Stephen*, and how *Peter Receives the Gospel of Grace*.

The *Missionary Journeys of Paul* takes an in-depth look at Paul's three journeys based on the specific Scripture readings in the Book of Acts.

Chronology of Paul's Journeys and Imprisonments

Paul at Damascus	37 – 40 AD
First Journey	45 – 47 AD
Second Journey	51 – 53 AD
Third Journey	54 – 58 AD
Imprisonment at Judea	58 – 60 AD
Voyage to Rome	60 – 61 AD
Imprisonment in Rome	61 – 63 AD
Post-Imprisonment Journeys	63 – 67 AD

[10] *McGee, Matthew. "Chronology of Apostle Paul's Journeys and Epistles."*

Covenants:
I will be their *God*
and they will be
my people.

Revelations 21:7 (CEV)

God's Covenants

The Abrahamic Covenant

God promised Abraham that he would be a father of many nations, very fruitful, given the promised land (Israel), and kings would descend from him. God told Abraham, *[10]"This is my covenant, which you shall keep, between me and you and your offspring after you: Every male among you shall be circumcised. [11]You shall be circumcised in the flesh of your foreskins, and it shall be a sign of the covenant between me and you"* (Genesis 17:10 – 11, ESV).

God's covenant with Abraham was for all nations to know God from the offspring of Abraham. Jesus was a direct descendant of Abraham and David. All believers in Jesus are called the seed of Abraham.

The promises to Abraham and his future descendants did not come through adhering to the Law, but through the righteousness that comes by having faith in God (Romans 4:13).

When a person accepts Jesus as Lord and Savior, he or she is granted the same promises as Abraham. "And now that you belong to Christ, you are the true children of Abraham. You are his heirs, and God's promise to Abraham belongs to you" (Galatians 3:29, NLT). Therefore, if children, then heirs of God and fellow heirs with Jesus. We share in His sufferings, in order, to share in the inheritance of His glory (Romans 8:17).

The Old Covenant (Mosaic Law or Law of Moses)

After God freed the Israelites from under Pharaoh's control, Moses led them into the wilderness of Sinai. God called to Moses from the mountain and said, *[5]"Now if you obey me fully and keep my covenant, then out of all nations you will be my treasured possession (chosen people). Although, the whole earth is mine, [6]you will be for me a kingdom of priests and a holy nation. These are the words you are to speak to the Israelites"* (Exodus 19:5 – 6).

God called Israel to be a holy nation who worshiped and had faith in the one and true, living God. The Israelites agreed to this covenant with God to obey the Mosaic Law (Ten Commandments).

The reason for the Mosaic Law was to make Israel aware of their sins. "Therefore, no one will be justified in His sight by works of the Law. For the Law merely brings awareness of sin" (Romans 3:20, BSB).

Jesus was sent to earth not to destroy the Law, but to fulfill the Law (Matthew 5:17) and make a New Covenant between God and His people.

THE LAW:	SALVATION:
• JUSTIFIED BY WORKS	• JUSTIFIED BY FAITH
• BY MEANS OF THE FLESH (SELF)	• BY MEANS OF THE SPIRIT (GRACE)
• AWARENESS OF SINS	• REPENTANCE OF SINS
• PUNISHMENT	• FORGIVENESS
• RULES	• RELATIONSHIP
• GUARDIAN	• CHILD OF GOD
• ATONEMENT OF SINS	• ONE IN CHRIST

The New Covenant (the Gospel of Grace)

Paul said the purpose of the Mosaic Law was to identify transgressions until the seed (Jesus) came to fulfill God's new covenant promise. The Mosaic Law required the sacrifice of animals for the atonement of sins until God sent his Son Jesus. God fulfilled all of His covenant promises in the Old Testament through Jesus Christ.

The Law or law-keeping does not save us but directs us to Christ for our salvation and our righteousness. [24] "Let me put it another way. The law was our guardian until Christ came; it protected us until we could be made right with God through faith. [25]And now that the way of faith has come, we no longer need the law as our guardian. [26]For you are all children of God through faith in Christ Jesus" (Galatians 3:24 – 26, NLT).

I never questioned the reason for taking communion at church as a new Christian. I did not understand its significance in that it represents the new covenant between God and His believers, as Jesus so eloquently stated at the table of the Last Supper. [14]"When the hour came, Jesus and his apostles reclined at the table. [15]And he said to them, *"I have eagerly desired to eat this Passover with you before I suffer. [16]For I tell you, I will not eat it again until it finds fulfillment in the kingdom of God. [17]"After taking the cup, he gave thanks and said, "Take this and divide it among you. [18]For I tell you I will not drink again from the fruit of the vine until the kingdom of God comes."*

[19]And he took bread, gave thanks and broke it, and gave it to them, saying, *"This is my body given for you; do this in remembrance of me."* [20]In the same way, after the supper he took the cup, saying, *"This cup is the new covenant in my blood, which is poured out for you"* (Luke 22:14 – 20).

"As the first Passover marked the Hebrews' release from Egyptian slavery, so the death of Christ marks our release from the slavery of sin (Romans 8:2). As the first Passover was to be held in remembrance as an annual feast, so Christians are to memorialize the Lord's death in communion until He returns (1 Corinthians 11:26).

The Old Testament Passover lamb, although a reality in that time, was a mere foreshadowing of the better and final Passover Lamb, Jesus Christ. Through His sinless life and sacrificial death, Jesus became the only One capable of giving people a way to escape death and a sure hope of eternal life" (1 Peter 1:20 – 21). [11]

The Christian Movement

The crucifixion, resurrection, and ascension of Jesus took place in the spring of 32 A.D. The Book of Acts is a continuation of Jesus's teachings and the power of the Holy Spirit working through the Church.

³"After his suffering, he (Jesus) presented himself to them (Apostles) and gave many convincing proofs that he was alive. He appeared to them over a period of forty days and spoke about the kingdom of God (heaven). ⁴On one occasion, while he was eating with them, he gave them this command: *"Do not leave Jerusalem, but wait for the gift my Father promised, which you have heard me speak about. ⁵For John baptized with water, but in a few days, you will be baptized with the Holy Spirit"* (Acts 1:3 – 5).

The Apostles had been witnesses of Jesus's death and resurrection. Jesus told them, *"But you will receive power when the Holy Spirit has come upon you, and you will be my witnesses in Jerusalem and in all Judea and Samaria, and to the end of the earth"* (Acts 1:8). After Jesus had ascended into heaven, the second time, the Apostles together with the women and Mary, the mother of Jesus, and his brothers returned to the upper room and prayed in obedience and supplication according to the Scriptures and the will of God.

The Day of Pentecost – Acts 2

¹When the day of Pentecost came, they were all together in one place.² Suddenly a sound like the blowing of a violent wind came from heaven and filled the whole house where they were sitting. ³ They saw what *seemed* to be tongues of fire that separated and came to rest on each of them. ⁴All of them were filled with the Holy Spirit and began to speak in other tongues as the Spirit enabled them.

⁵ Now there were staying in Jerusalem God-fearing Jews from every nation under heaven. ⁶ When they heard this sound, a crowd came together in bewilderment, because each one heard their own language being spoken. ⁷ Utterly amazed, they asked: "Aren't all these who are speaking, Galileans? ⁸ Then how is it that each of us hears them in our native language? ⁹ Parthians, Medes and Elamites; residents of Mesopotamia, Judea and Cappadocia, Pontus and Asia, ¹⁰ Phrygia and Pamphylia, Egypt and the parts of Libya near

Old (First) Covenant	New (Last) Covenant
Garden of Eden	Garden of Gethsemane
Tree of Life	Christ Hung on a Tree
First Adam (death)	Last Adam (life)
Israel	Church
Saved from Egypt	Saved from Hell
Crossed the Red Sea	Baptized into the Body
First Passover	Christ our Passover
Manna from Heaven	Jesus the Bread of Life
Law from Moses	Grace & Truth from Christ
Physical Weapons & Fight	Spiritual Weapons & Fight
Rest in the Promised Land	Rest in Heaven

Cyrene; visitors from Rome ¹¹ (both Jews and converts to Judaism); Cretans and Arabs—we hear them declaring the wonders of God in our own tongues!"

¹²Amazed and perplexed, they asked one another, "What does this mean?" ¹³ Some, however, made fun of them and said, "They have had too much wine."

¹⁴Then Peter stood up with the Eleven, raised his voice and addressed the crowd: "Fellow Jews and all of you who live in Jerusalem, let me explain this to you; listen carefully to what I say. ¹⁵ These people are not drunk, as you suppose. It's only nine in the morning! ¹⁶ No, this is what was spoken by the prophet Joel:

¹⁷ "In the last days, God says,
    I will pour out my Spirit on all people.
    Your sons and daughters will prophesy,
    your young men will see visions,
    your old men will dream dreams.
¹⁸ Even on my servants, both men and women,
    I will pour out my Spirit in those days,
    and they will prophesy.
¹⁹ I will show wonders in the heavens above
    and signs on the earth below,
    blood and fire and billows of smoke.
²⁰ The sun will be turned to darkness
    and the moon to blood
    before the coming of the great and glorious day of the Lord.
²¹ And everyone who calls
    on the name of the Lord will be saved.'

²² "Fellow Israelites, listen to this: Jesus of Nazareth was a man accredited by God to you by miracles, wonders and signs, which God did among you through him, as you yourselves know. ²³ This man was handed over to you by God's deliberate plan and foreknowledge; and you, with the help of wicked men, put him to death by nailing him to the cross. ²⁴ But God raised him from the dead, freeing him from

the agony of death, because it was impossible for death to keep its hold on him" (Act 2:1-24).

[36]*"Therefore let all Israel be assured of this: God has made this Jesus, whom you crucified, both Lord and Messiah."* [37] When the people heard this, they were cut to the heart and said to Peter and the other apostles, *"Brothers, what shall we do?"* [38] Peter replied, *"Repent and be baptized, every one of you, in the name of Jesus Christ for the forgiveness of your sins. And you will receive the gift of the Holy Spirit. [39] The promise is for you and your children and for all who are far off—for all whom the Lord our God will call."*

[40] With many other words he warned them; and he pleaded with them, "Save yourselves from this corrupt generation." [41] Those who accepted his message were baptized, and about three thousand were added to their number that day.

[42] They devoted themselves to the apostles' teaching and to fellowship, to the breaking of bread and to prayer. [43] Everyone was filled with awe at the many wonders and signs performed by the apostles. [44] All the believers were together and had everything in common. [45] They sold property and possessions to give to anyone who had need. [46] Every day they continued to meet together in the temple courts. They broke bread in their homes and ate together with glad and sincere hearts, [47] praising God and enjoying the favor of all the people. And the Lord added to their number daily those who were being saved" (Acts 2:36 – 47).

The Story of Stephen

[8]"Now Stephen, a man full of God's grace and power, performed great wonders and signs among the people. [9]Opposition arose, however, from members of the Synagogue of the Freedmen (as it was called)—Jews of Cyrene and Alexandria as well as the provinces of Cilicia and Asia—who began to argue with Stephen. [10]But they could not stand up against the wisdom the Spirit gave him as he spoke" (Acts 6:8 – 10).

[11]"Then, they secretly persuaded some men to say, *"We have heard*

Stephen speak blasphemous words against Moses and against God." [12]So, they stirred up the people and the elders and the teachers of the law. They seized Stephen and brought him before the Sanhedrin" (Acts 6:11 – 12). [13]"They produced false witnesses, who testified, "This fellow never stops speaking against this holy place and against the law. [14]For we have heard him say that this Jesus of Nazareth will destroy this place and change the customs Moses handed down to us." [15]All who were sitting in the Sanhedrin looked intently at Stephen, and they saw that his face was like the face of an angel (Acts 6:13 – 15).

Stephen began his testimony by stating that Israel had always rejected the truth. You rejected Abraham. You rejected Moses. You rejected Joseph. You rejected Jesus. Now, you reject me. [51]"*You stiff-necked people! Your hearts and ears are still uncircumcised. You are just like your ancestors: You always resist the Holy Spirit!* [52]*Was there ever a prophet your ancestors did not persecute? They even killed those who predicted the coming of the Righteous One. And now you have betrayed and murdered him—* [53]*you who have received the law that was given through angels but have not obeyed it*" (Acts 7:51 – 53).

The Sanhedrin became so enraged by Stephen's speech they started gnashing their teeth at him. But, Stephen, full of the Holy Spirit, looked up and saw the glory of God and said, *"Behold, I see the heavens opened and the Son of Man standing at the right hand of God"* (Acts 7:56, WEB). [57]"But they cried out with a loud voice and stopped their ears and rushed together at him. [58]Then they cast him out of the city and stoned him. And the witnesses laid down their garments at the feet of a young man named Saul. [59]And as they were stoning Stephen, he called out, *"Lord Jesus, receive my spirit."* [60]And falling to his knees, he cried out with a loud voice, *"Lord, do not hold this sin against them."* And when he had said this, he fell asleep" (Acts 7:57 – 60, ESV).

[1]"And Saul approved of his execution.

And there arose on that day a great persecution against the church in Jerusalem, and they were all scattered throughout the regions of Judea and Samaria, except the apostles. [2]Devout men buried Stephen and made great lamentation over him. ³But Saul was ravaging the church, and entering house after house, he dragged off men and women and committed them to prison" (Acts 8:1 – 3, ESV).

Peter receives the Gospel of Grace

The Apostle Peter traveled throughout all parts of the country in his ministry performing miracles in the name of the Lord. When he reached Joppa, he *lodged* several days at the home of a Tanner named Simon (Acts 9:43). According to the Jewish laws, it was strictly forbidden to associate with anyone who worked with dead animals, especially a Tanner, because of the constant uncleanliness. When Peter returned to Jerusalem, he shared with others what had happened in Joppa.

¹ Soon the news reached the apostles and other believers in Judea that the Gentiles had received the word of God. ² But when Peter arrived back in Jerusalem, the Jewish believers criticized him. ³ "You entered the home of Gentiles and even ate with them!" they said.

⁴ Then Peter told them exactly what had happened. ⁵ "I was in the town of Joppa," he said, "and while I was praying, I went into a trance and saw a vision. Something like a large sheet was let down by its four corners from the sky. And it came right down to me. ⁶ When I looked inside the sheet, I saw all sorts of tame and wild animals, reptiles, and birds. ⁷ And I heard a voice say, 'Get up, Peter; kill and eat them.'

⁸ "'No, Lord,' I replied. 'I have never eaten anything that our Jewish laws have declared impure or unclean.'

⁹ "But the voice from heaven spoke again: 'Do not call something unclean if God has made it clean.' ¹⁰ This happened three times before the sheet and all it contained was pulled back up to heaven.

¹¹ "Just then three (Gentile) men who had been sent (by Cornelius) from Caesarea arrived at the (Tanner Simon's) house where we were staying. ¹² The Holy Spirit told me to go with them and not to worry that they were Gentiles. These six brothers here accompanied me, and we soon entered the home of the man (Cornelius) who had sent

for us. ¹³ He told us how an angel had appeared to him in his home and had told him, 'Send messengers to Joppa, and summon a man named Simon Peter. ¹⁴ He will tell you how you and everyone in your household can be saved!'

¹⁵ "As I began to speak," Peter continued, "the Holy Spirit fell on them, just as he fell on us at the beginning. ¹⁶ Then I thought of the Lord's words when he said, 'John baptized with water, but you will be baptized with the Holy Spirit.' ¹⁷ And since God gave these Gentiles the same gift he gave us when we believed in the Lord Jesus Christ, who was I to stand in God's way?"

¹⁸ When the others heard this, they stopped objecting and began praising God. They said, "We can see that God has also given the Gentiles the privilege of repenting of their sins and receiving eternal life."

¹⁹ "Meanwhile, the believers who had been scattered during the

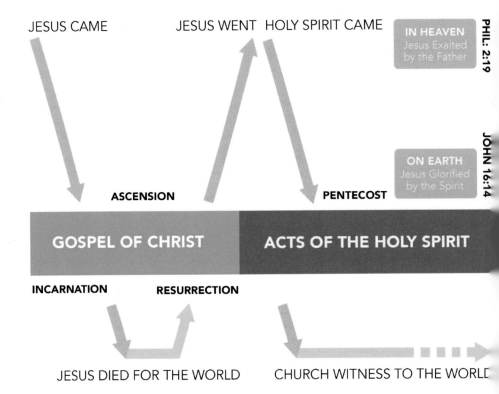

persecution after Stephen's death traveled as far as Phoenicia, Cyprus, and Antioch of Syria. They preached the word of God, but only to Jews.[20] However, some of the believers who went to Antioch from Cyprus and Cyrene began preaching to the Gentiles about the Lord Jesus. [21] The power of the Lord was with them, and a large number of these Gentiles believed and turned to the Lord.

[22] When the church at Jerusalem heard what had happened, they sent Barnabas to Antioch. [23] When he arrived and saw this evidence of God's blessing, he was filled with joy, and he encouraged the believers to stay true to the Lord. [24] Barnabas was a good man, full of the Holy Spirit and strong in faith. And many people were brought to the Lord" (Acts 11:1-24 NLT).

THE MISSIONARY JOURNEYS OF PAUL

The First Missionary Journey (45 – 47 A.D.)

After Paul had fled from Damascus, he was sent by the Apostles to live in Tarsus. Paul was still residing in Tarsus when the church members in Jerusalem sent Barnabas to (Syrian) Antioch to build up a church and lead the congregation. [25] "Then Barnabas went to Tarsus to look for Paul, [26] and when he found him, he brought him to Antioch. So for a whole year Barnabas and Paul met with the church and taught great numbers of people. Disciples were called Christians first at Antioch" (Acts 11:25 – 26).

One day when Barnabas and Paul were worshipping and fasting, the Holy Spirit said to them, separate unto God and fulfill the specific work that God has called you to do. Then, the prophets at Antioch laid hands upon Barnabas and Paul and sent them away on their first missionary journey. John Mark, Barnabas' cousin, also went with them as their assistant.

They preached in the Jewish Synagogues in the cities of Seleucia, Salamis, and Paphos. Upon their arrival at Paphos, they met a false prophet named Elymas who was with the Proconsul, Sergius Paulus.

So for a whole year *Barnabas* and *Saul* met with the *church* and *taught* great numbers of people. The disciples were called *Christians first at Antioch.*

Acts 11:26 (KJB)

The proconsul was responsible for the province and for answering to the Roman Senate. Paulus requested to hear the word of God from Barnabas and Paul.

⁸But Elymas, the sorcerer, opposed them and tried to turn the proconsul from the faith. ⁹Then Saul, who was also called Paul, filled with the Holy Spirit, looked straight at Elymas and said, ¹⁰ *"You are a child of the devil and an enemy of everything that is right! You are full of all kinds of deceit and trickery. Will you never stop perverting the right ways of the Lord?* ¹¹ *Now the hand of the Lord is against you. You are going to be blind for a time, not even able to see the light of the sun."* ¹²Immediately mist and darkness came over him, and he groped about, seeking someone to lead him by the hand. When the proconsul saw what had happened, he believed, for he was amazed at the teaching about the Lord (Acts 13:8 – 12).

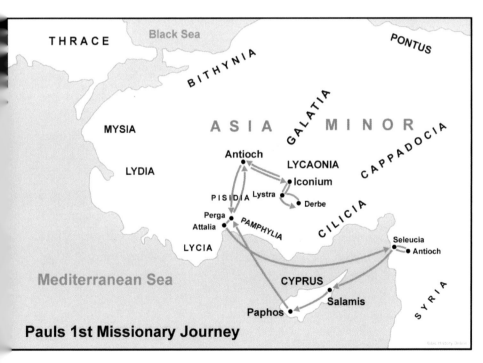

Pauls 1st Missionary Journey

Image (above): Map of the locations visited by Paul on his first missionary journey. Reprinted courtesy of: https://www.bible-history.com/new-testament/pauls-first-missionary-journey.html

Next, they sailed to Perga (Turkey) in Pamphylia where John Mark departed from them and returned to Jerusalem. From Perga, they went to the synagogue in Pisidian Antioch. Paul spoke on Israel's history. He began with the story of Abraham and his descendants, the deliverance out of Egypt, the forty years in the wilderness, the defeat of Canaan, the period of the Judges, the establishment of kings, and how it all led up to the birth and resurrection of Jesus.

Paul said, [38] *"Therefore, my friends, I want you to know that through Jesus the forgiveness of sins is proclaimed to you.* [39] *Through him everyone who believes is set free from every sin, a justification you were not able to obtain under the Law of Moses"* (Acts 13:38 – 39). The people were intrigued and invited him to speak further about these things on the next Sabbath.

The following Sabbath, the people of the city, gathered in the synagogue to hear Paul preach. When the Jews saw the large crowd, they became jealous, contradicted Paul, blasphemed Jesus, and expelled them from the region. [46] *"Then Paul and Barnabas answered them boldly: "We had to speak the word of God to you first. Since you reject it and do not consider yourselves worthy of eternal life, we now turn to the Gentiles.* [47] *For this is what the Lord has commanded us: "I have made you a light for the Gentiles, that you may bring salvation to the ends of the earth."* [48] When the Gentiles heard this, they were glad and honored the word of the Lord; and all who were appointed for eternal life believed.

[49] The word of the Lord spread through the whole region. [50] But the Jewish leaders incited the God-fearing women of high standing and the leading men of the city. They stirred up persecution against Paul and Barnabas and expelled them from their region. [51] So they shook the dust off their feet as a warning to them and went to Iconium. [52] And the disciples were filled with joy and with the Holy Spirit" (Acts 13:46 – 52).

[1]"At Iconium Paul and Barnabas went as usual into the Jewish synagogue. There they spoke so effectively that a great number of Jews and Greeks believed. [2] But the Jews who refused to believe stirred up the other Gentiles and poisoned their minds against the brothers. [3] So

And by Him all that *believe* are *justified* from all things, from which ye could NOT be justified by the *law of Moses*.

Acts 13:39 (KJB)

Paul and Barnabas spent considerable time there, speaking boldly for the Lord, who confirmed the message of his grace by enabling them to perform signs and wonders. [4] The people of the city were divided; some sided with the Jews, others with the apostles. [5] There was a plot afoot among both Gentiles and Jews, together with their leaders, to mistreat them and stone them. [6] But they found out about it and fled to the Lycaonian cities of Lystra and Derbe and to the surrounding country, [7] where they continued to preach the gospel" (Acts 14:1 – 7).

While Paul was preaching the gospel in Lystra, a lame man had faith and became healed. The crowd, who witnessed the healing, declared Paul and Barnabas to be the gods, Zeus and Hermes. Then, the priest of Zeus brought garland and oxen to make a sacrificial offering to Paul and Barnabas. Paul rebuked them and told them to turn away from this pagan worship and instead, worship the one, true living God. The crowd would not listen and continued to make the sacrifices to them.

[19] Then some Jews came from Antioch and Iconium and won the crowd over. They stoned Paul and dragged him outside the city, thinking he was dead. [20] But after the disciples had gathered around him, he got up and went back into the city. The next day he and Barnabas left for Derbe. [21] They preached the gospel in that city and won a large number of disciples.

Then they returned to Lystra, Iconium and Antioch, [22] strengthening the disciples and encouraging them to remain true to the faith. "*We must go through many hardships to enter the kingdom of God*," they said. [23] Paul and Barnabas appointed elders for them in each church and, with prayer and fasting, committed them to the Lord, in whom they had put their trust. [24] After going through Pisidia, they came into Pamphylia, [25] and when they had preached the word in Perga, they went down to Attalia.

[26] From Attalia they sailed back to (Syrian) Antioch, where they had been committed to the grace of God for the work they had now completed. [27] On arriving there, they gathered the church together and reported all that God had done through them and how he had

opened a door of faith to the Gentiles. [28] And they stayed there a long time with the disciples (Acts 14:19 – 28).

The Jerusalem Council's Decision (49 – 50 A.D.)

Some Jewish Christians from Judea came to visit the church at Antioch. They told the congregation that the Gentiles had to become Jews first (circumcised) before they could become a Christian. *"Unless you are circumcised, according to the custom taught by Moses, you cannot be saved"* (Acts 15:1). Paul and Barnabas disagreed with this reasoning and debated with these men. The church appointed Paul and Barnabas along with some other believers to visit Jerusalem and ask the council, comprised of apostles and elders, about the question of circumcision.

When Paul and Barnabas arrived in Jerusalem, the church and the council welcomed them. They reported everything God had done during their first missionary journey. They told the council about establishing churches among the Gentiles without requiring that they follow the Law of Moses. The men from Judea said that Paul and Barnabas were wrong by not making the Gentiles keep and obey the Law. [5]"Then some of the believers who belonged to the party of the Pharisees stood up and said, "*The Gentiles must be circumcised and required to keep the Law of Moses*" (Acts 15:5). After this statement, the council had a meeting to discuss the matter further.

Peter addressed the council stating that God knows and purifies the heart by faith. After Peter's experience in Joppa, he declared that God does not discriminate between the Jews and Gentiles. Peter said it is through the grace of our Lord Jesus that we become saved, just as we are. He accepts all who believe by giving them the Holy Spirit, just as he did to us. [10] "Now then, why do you try to test God by putting on the necks of Gentiles a yoke that neither we nor our ancestors have been able to bear? [11] No! We believe it is through the grace of our Lord Jesus that we are saved, just as they are" (Acts 15:10 – 11).

Paul and Barnabas told the council about the signs and wonders that God did through them among the Gentiles. When they finished,

James said, [19]*"It is my judgment, therefore, that we should not make it difficult for the Gentiles who are turning to God. [20]Instead we should write to them, telling them to abstain from food polluted by idols, from sexual immorality, from the meat of strangled animals and from blood. [21]For the law of Moses has been preached in every city from the earliest times and is read in the synagogues on every Sabbath"* (Acts 15:19 – 21). James made this request out of respect for the Jewish traditions because the Law of Moses was still being preached in every city and read in the synagogues on every Sabbath.

The council decided the matter and wrote a letter to the churches. They sent two leaders from their congregation, Judas, and Silas, along with Paul and Barnabas with the letter to Antioch. They addressed the letter from the apostles, elders, and brothers *to the Gentile believers* in Antioch, Syria, and Cilicia. The letter stated the following:

Greetings,

[24]"We have heard that some went out from us without our authorization and disturbed you, troubling your minds by what they said. [25] So we all agreed to choose some men and send them to you with our dear friends Barnabas and Paul— [26] men who have risked their lives for the name of our Lord Jesus Christ. [27] Therefore we are sending Judas and Silas to confirm by word of mouth what we are writing. [28] It seemed good to the Holy Spirit and to us not to burden you with anything beyond the following requirements: [29] You are to abstain from food sacrificed to idols, from blood, from the meat of strangled animals and from sexual immorality. You will do well to avoid these things.

Farewell"

(Acts 15:24 – 29)

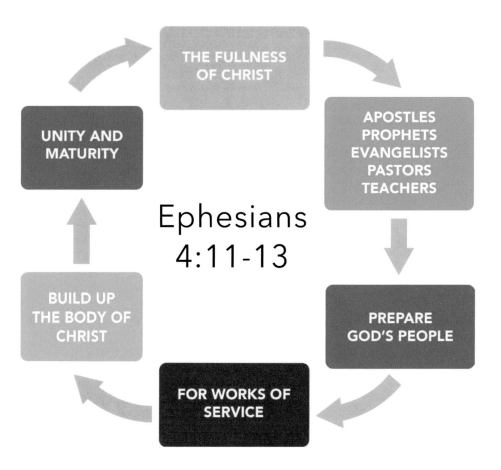

The Gentile and Jewish Christians were glad and in agreement with the council's decision regarding non-circumcision, abstaining from certain foods, and holding one another accountable. Judas and Silas stayed in Antioch for a while to encourage and strengthen the believers with the message of peace. Paul and Barnabas continued to teach and preach the word of God in Antioch. Approximately five years later, Paul said to Barnabas, [36]"*Let us go back and visit the believers in all the towns where we preached the word of the Lord and see how they are doing.*"

[37]Barnabas wanted to take John, also called Mark, with them, [38]but

Paul did not think it wise to take him, because he had deserted them in Pamphylia and had not continued with them in the work. [39] They had such a sharp disagreement that they parted company. Barnabas took Mark and sailed for Cyprus, [40] but Paul chose Silas and left, commended by the believers to the grace of the Lord. [41] He went through Syria and Cilicia, strengthening the churches" (Acts 15:36 – 41).

The Second Missionary Journey (51 – 53 A.D.)

Paul and Silas went through Syria and Cilicia on the second missionary journey to revisit and strengthen the established churches. They decided to visit Lystra, the city where the people initially wanted to worship Paul and Barnabas as gods, became angry with them, and then wanted to stone them to death. When they arrived in Lystra, they met a disciple named Timothy. His mother was a believing Jew, and his father was a Greek. The brethren spoke highly of Timothy. Paul invited him to join their journey.

Since Timothy was considered a half-Jew, Paul decided, out of love for the believing Jews in that region, to circumcise Timothy. Paul, respectfully, decided to circumcise Timothy because he did not want this to be an issue among the brethren, hinder their ministry, or their opportunity to teach and preach in the synagogues. As Paul, Silas, and Timothy traveled throughout the regions, they delivered the Jerusalem Council's decrees to the churches. The people were encouraged in the faith, and the churches grew daily in numbers.

Originally, Paul had planned to travel through the province of Asia to Ephesus, but the Holy Spirit redirected him to Troas to pick up Luke and journey toward Europe. This effort was the first missionary attempt to Europe by man. That night Paul had a vision of a Macedonian man begging him to help them in Macedonia. Paul told the others that God wanted them to preach the gospel in this region.

Therefore, sailing from Troas, they headed toward Samothrace,

Neapolis, and then stopped in Philippi to establish a church in this major city. The city did not have a synagogue or many Jews living there. On the Sabbath day, they went to the riverside where the people prayed. Paul met a woman named Lydia. She sold expensive purple cloth in Philippi. Lydia's heart responded to Paul's message. She and her household became baptized. Lydia persuaded Paul and the others to come and stay at her house. They agreed to stay in her home.

The Imprisoned Story

Acts 16 is narrated by Luke. [16] "Once when we were going to the place of prayer, we were met by a female slave who had a spirit by which she predicted the future. She earned a great deal of money for her owners by fortune-telling. [17] She followed Paul and the rest of us, shouting, "These men are servants of the Most High God, who are telling you the way to be saved." [18] She kept this up for many days. Finally, Paul became so annoyed that he turned around and said to

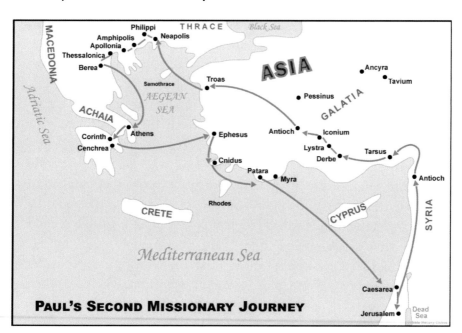

Image (above): Map of the locations visited by Paul on his second missionary journey. Reprinted courtesy of: www.bible-history.com

the spirit, "In the name of Jesus Christ I command you to come out of her!" At that moment, the spirit left her.

[19] When her owners realized that their hope of making money was gone, they seized Paul and Silas and dragged them into the marketplace to face the authorities. [20] They brought them before the magistrates and said, "These men are Jews, and are throwing our city into an uproar [21] by advocating customs unlawful for us Romans to accept or practice."

[22] The crowd joined in the attack against Paul and Silas, and the magistrates ordered them to be stripped and beaten with rods. [23] After they had been severely flogged, they were thrown into prison, and the jailer was commanded to guard them carefully. [24] When he received these orders, he put them in the inner cell and fastened their feet in the stocks.

[25] About midnight Paul and Silas were praying and singing hymns to God, and the other prisoners were listening to them. [26] Suddenly there was such a violent earthquake that the foundations of the prison were shaken. At once all the prison doors flew open, and everyone's chains came loose. [27] The jailer woke up, and when he saw the prison doors open, he drew his sword and was about to kill himself because he thought the prisoners had escaped. [28] But Paul shouted, "Don't harm yourself! We are all here!"

[29] The jailer called for lights, rushed in and fell trembling before Paul and Silas. [30] He then brought them out and asked, "Sirs, what must I do to be saved?"

[31] They replied, "Believe in the Lord Jesus, and you will be saved— you and your household." [32] Then they spoke the word of the Lord to him and to all the others in his house. [33] At that hour of the night the jailer took them and washed their wounds; then immediately he and all his household were baptized. [34] The jailer brought them into his house and set a meal before them; he was filled with joy because he had come to believe in God—he and his whole household. [35] When it was daylight, the magistrates sent their officers to the jailer with the order: "Release those men." [36] The jailer told Paul, "The magistrates have ordered that you and Silas be released. Now you can leave. Go

in peace."

[37] But Paul said to the officers: "They beat us publicly without a trial, even though we are Roman citizens, and threw us into prison. And now do they want to get rid of us quietly? No! Let them come themselves and escort us out."

[38] The officers reported this to the magistrates, and when they heard that Paul and Silas were Roman citizens, they were alarmed. [39] They came to appease them and escorted them from the prison, requesting them to leave the city. [40] After Paul and Silas came out of the prison, they went to Lydia's house, where they met with the brothers and sisters and encouraged them. Then they left" (Acts 16:16 – 40). But, Luke stayed in Philippi to help build up the new congregation.

Thessalonica, Berea, and Athens

Paul, Silas, and Timothy passed through Amphipolis and Apollonia to get to Thessalonica, where there was a Jewish Synagogue. Paul preached the Scriptures for three Sabbaths in the synagogue "[3]explaining and proving that the Messiah had to suffer and rise from the dead. "This Jesus I am proclaiming to you is the Messiah," he said.[4] Some of the Jews were persuaded and joined Paul and Silas, as did a large number of God-fearing Greeks and quite a few prominent women" (Acts 17:3 – 4).

A mob of the non-believing Jews became jealous and created havoc in the city. The crowd went to Jason's house looking for Paul and Silas. They could not find them, so they dragged Jason and the brethren that were with him before the city officials. They yelled out, *"These men who have caused trouble all over the world have now come here, [7] and Jason has welcomed them into his house. They are all defying Caesar's decrees, saying that there is another king, one called Jesus."* [8] When they heard this, the crowd and the city officials were thrown into turmoil. [9] Then they made Jason and the others post bond and let them go (Acts 17:6- 9). Soon after, the brethren sent Paul and Silas away during the night to Berea.

The people of Berea readily received Paul, Silas, Timothy, and the Word of God. They preached in the Jewish Synagogue, and the Bereans diligently searched the Scriptures daily to understand their teachings. Many of the people believed. When the Jews from Thessalonica heard that Paul and Silas were preaching in Berea, they came to that city to stir up the crowds. Paul left immediately by sea to Athens while Silas and Timothy remained in Berea to teach and build up the new church.

Paul's spirit was heavy when he discovered that the people of Athens were involved in idol worship. There were different types of idols scattered throughout the city for the people to worship. Paul began teaching the Jews and Gentiles that he met in the synagogue and the marketplace about the resurrected Son of God.

Some Epicurean and Stoic philosophers heard Paul teaching and out of curiosity invited him to speak on Areopagus Hill in the intellectual part of the city. They wanted to learn more about this new doctrine that their ears had never heard. Paul stood in the middle of the Areopagus and began his lecture.

He said I see that you are very religious. You have all of these idols placed throughout the city. I even found an altar inscribed "*To an Unknown God.*" (The people of Athens even worshipped idols that were unidentifiable or unknown). To pique their intellectual curiosity, Paul told the philosophers that the "unknown God" whom you do not even know and worship, I proclaim to you is the *one true living God.*

Paul said, [24] "The God who made the world and everything in it is the Lord of heaven and earth and does not live in temples built by human hands.[25] And he is not served by human hands, as if he needed anything. Rather, he himself gives everyone life and breath and everything else.[26] From one man he made all the nations, that they should inhabit the whole earth; and he marked out their appointed times in history and the boundaries of their lands. [27] God did this so that they would seek him and perhaps reach out for him and find him, though he is not far from any one of us. [28] '*For in him we live and move and have our being.*' As some of your own poets have said, '*We are his offspring.*'

²⁹ "Therefore since we are God's offspring, we should not think that the divine being is like gold or silver or stone—an image made by human design and skill. ³⁰ In the past God overlooked such ignorance, but now he commands all people everywhere to repent. ³¹ For he has set a day when he will judge the world with justice by the man he has appointed. He has given proof of this to everyone by raising him from the dead."

³² When they heard about the resurrection of the dead, some of them sneered, but others said, "We want to hear you again on this subject."³³ At that, Paul left the Council. ³⁴ Some of the people became followers of Paul and believed. Among them was Dionysius, a member of the Areopagus, also a woman named Damaris, and a number of others" (Acts 17:24 – 34). Paul later departed from Athens and went to Corinth.

Corinth

Paul met a married couple in Corinth named Aquila and Priscilla ³"and because he was a tentmaker as they were, he stayed and worked with them. ⁴Every Sabbath he reasoned in the synagogue, trying to persuade Jews and Greeks. ⁵When Silas and Timothy came from Macedonia, Paul devoted himself exclusively to preaching, testifying to the Jews that Jesus was the Messiah. ⁶But when they opposed Paul and became abusive, he shook out his clothes in protest and said to them, *"Your blood be on your own heads! I am innocent of it. From now on I will go to the Gentiles."*

⁷Then Paul left the synagogue and went next door to the house of Titius Justus, a worshiper of God. ⁸Crispus, the synagogue leader, and his entire household believed in the Lord; and many of the Corinthians who heard Paul believed and were baptized" (Acts 18:3 – 8).

One night, the Lord came to Paul in a vision and encouraged him not to be afraid, but to continue to preach because no harm would come to him in this city. Paul remained in Corinth for a year and a half teaching the word of God to the people.

For in *Him* we live and move and have *our being*... we are His offspring.

Acts 17:28 (NIV)

When Gallio became the proconsul of Achaia, the non-believing Jews brought Paul before the judgment-seat. They charged Paul with persuading the people to worship God in ways contrary to the law. Before Paul could even speak, Gallio said this is not a matter of crime but involves your words and your religious rules. Gallio told them that he would not judge such things. He instructed them to solve these matters themselves. Then, the crowd turned on the synagogue leader, Sosthenes, and beat him in front of Gallio, who left and could care less.

Paul stayed in Corinth a little while longer, took the Nazirite vow (to abstain from eating or drinking products made from the grapevine, from going near dead bodies, and he cut off all of his hair) before sailing to Syria with Aquila and Priscilla. When they arrived at Ephesus, Paul left Aquila and Priscilla there. "When he had landed at Caesarea, he went up to Jerusalem and greeted the church and then went down to Antioch" (Acts 18:22). He spent considerable time there and then left again.

The Third Missionary Journey (54 – 58 A.D.)

Paul began his third missionary journey at Syrian Antioch. The reason for his travels was to strengthen and encourage the existing churches and to seek donations for the poor Christians living in Jerusalem. He went from one place to the next through the region of Galatia and Phrygia, including Tarsus, Derbe, Lystra, Iconium, and Pisidian Antioch.

[1]"Paul took the road through the interior and arrived at Ephesus. There he found some disciples [2]and asked them, "Did you receive the Holy Spirit when you believed?" They answered, "No, we have not even heard that there is a Holy Spirit." [3] So Paul asked, "Then what baptism did you receive?" "John's baptism," they replied.

[4] Paul said, "John's baptism was a baptism of repentance. He told the people to believe in the one coming after him, that is, in Jesus." [5] On hearing this, they were baptized in the name of the Lord

Jesus. ⁶ When Paul placed his hands on them, the Holy Spirit came on them, and they spoke in tongues and prophesied. ⁷ There were about twelve men in all.

⁸ Paul entered the synagogue and spoke boldly there for three months, arguing persuasively about the kingdom of God. ⁹ But some of them became obstinate; they refused to believe and publicly maligned the Way. So Paul left them. He took the disciples with him and had discussions daily in the lecture hall of Tyrannus. ¹⁰ This went on for two years, so that all the Jews and Greeks who lived in the province of Asia heard the word of the Lord.

One night the Lord spoke to Paul in a vision: *Do not be afraid;* keep on speaking, do not be silent.

Acts 18:9 (NIV)

¹¹ God did extraordinary miracles through Paul, ¹² so that even handkerchiefs and aprons that had touched him were taken to the sick, and their illnesses were cured and the evil spirits left them.

¹³ Some Jews who went around driving out evil spirits tried to invoke the name of the Lord Jesus over those who were demon-possessed. They would say, "In the name of the Jesus whom Paul preaches, I command you to come out." ¹⁴ Seven sons of Sceva, a Jewish chief priest, were doing this. ¹⁵ One day the evil spirit answered them, "Jesus I know, and Paul I know about, but who are you?" ¹⁶ Then the man who had the evil spirit jumped on them and overpowered them all. He gave them such a beating that they ran out of the house naked and bleeding.

¹⁷ When this became known to the Jews and Greeks living in Ephesus, they were all seized with fear, and the name of the Lord Jesus was held in high honor. ¹⁸ Many of those who believed now

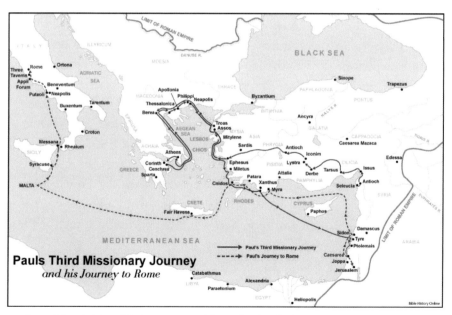

Image (above): Map of the locations visited by Paul on his third missionary journey, including his journey to Rome. Reprinted courtesy of: www.bible-history.com

came and openly confessed what they had done. ¹⁹ A number who had practiced sorcery brought their scrolls together and burned them publicly. When they calculated the value of the scrolls, the total came to fifty thousand drachmas. ²⁰ In this way the word of the Lord spread widely and grew in power" (Acts 19:1-20).

The Great Theater Riot

²³ "About that time there arose a great disturbance about the Way. ²⁴ A silversmith named Demetrius, who made silver shrines of Artemis, brought in a lot of business for the craftsmen there. ²⁵ He called them together, along with the workers in related trades, and said: "You know, my friends, that we receive a good income from this business. ²⁶ And you see and hear how this fellow Paul has convinced and led astray large numbers of people here in Ephesus and in practically the whole province of Asia. He says that gods made by human hands are no gods at all.²⁷ There is danger not only that our trade will lose its good name, but also that the temple of the great goddess Artemis will be discredited; and the goddess herself, who is worshiped throughout the province of Asia and the world, will be robbed of her divine majesty."

²⁸ When they heard this, they were furious and began shouting: "Great is Artemis of the Ephesians!" ²⁹ Soon the whole city was in an uproar. The people seized Gaius and Aristarchus, Paul's traveling companions from Macedonia, and all of them rushed into the theater together. ³⁰ Paul wanted to appear before the crowd, but the disciples would not let him.³¹ Even some of the officials of the province, friends of Paul, sent him a message begging him not to venture into the theater.

³² The assembly was in confusion: Some were shouting one thing, some another. Most of the people did not even know why they were there.³³ The Jews in the crowd pushed Alexander to the front, and they shouted instructions to him. He motioned for silence in order to make a defense before the people. ³⁴ But when they realized he was a Jew, they all shouted in unison for about two hours: "Great is

Artemis of the Ephesians!"

³⁵ The city clerk quieted the crowd and said: "Fellow Ephesians, doesn't all the world know that the city of Ephesus is the guardian of the temple of the great Artemis and of her image, which fell from heaven? ³⁶ Therefore, since these facts are undeniable, you ought to calm down and not do anything rash. ³⁷ You have brought these men here, though they have neither robbed temples nor blasphemed our goddess. ³⁸ If, then, Demetrius and his fellow craftsmen have a grievance against anybody, the courts are open and there are proconsuls. They can press charges. ³⁹ If there is anything further you want to bring up, it must be settled in a legal assembly. ⁴⁰ As it is, we are in danger of being charged with rioting because of what happened today. In that case we would not be able to account for this commotion, since there is no reason for it." ⁴¹ After he had said this, he dismissed the assembly" (Acts 19:23 – 41).

Macedonia, Greece, and Troas

¹"When the uproar had ended, Paul sent for the disciples and, after encouraging them, said goodbye and set out for Macedonia. ²He traveled through that area, speaking many words of encouragement to the people, and finally arrived in Greece, ³where he stayed for three months. Because some Jews had plotted against him just as he was about to sail for Syria, he decided to go back through Macedonia. ⁴He was accompanied by Sopater son of Pyrrhus from Berea, Aristarchus and Secundus from Thessalonica, Gaius from Derbe, Timothy also, and Tychicus and Trophimus from the province of Asia. ⁵These men went on ahead and waited for us (Luke and Paul) at Troas" (Acts 20:1 – 5).

⁶"But we (Luke and Paul) sailed from Philippi after the Festival of Unleavened Bread, and five days later joined the others at Troas, where we stayed seven days. ⁷On the first day of the week we came together to break bread. Paul spoke to the people and, because he intended to leave the next day, kept on talking until midnight. ⁸There were many lamps in the upstairs room where we were meeting. ⁹Seated

in a window was a young man named Eutychus, who was sinking into a deep sleep as Paul talked on and on. When he was sound asleep, he fell to the ground from the third story and was picked up dead. [10]Paul went down, threw himself on the young man and put his arms around him. "Don't be alarmed," he said. "He's alive!" [11]Then he went upstairs again and broke bread and ate. After talking until daylight, he left. [12]The people took the young man home alive and were greatly comforted" (Acts 20:6 – 12).

Paul says Goodbye to the Ephesian Elders

[16]"Paul had decided to sail past Ephesus to avoid spending time in the province of Asia, for he was in a hurry to reach Jerusalem, if possible, by the day of Pentecost. [17]From Miletus, Paul sent to Ephesus for the elders of the church.

[18]When they arrived, he said to them: "You know how I lived the whole time I was with you, from the first day I came into the province of Asia. [19]I served the Lord with great humility and with tears and in the midst of severe testing by the plots of my Jewish opponents. [20]You know that I have not hesitated to preach anything that would be helpful to you but have taught you publicly and from house to house. [21]I have declared to both Jews and Greeks that they must turn to God in repentance and have faith in our Lord Jesus."

[22]"And now, compelled by the Spirit, I am going to Jerusalem, not knowing what will happen to me there. [23]I only know that in every city the Holy Spirit warns me that prison and hardships are facing me. [24]However, I consider my life worth nothing to me; my only aim is to finish the race and complete the task the Lord Jesus has given me—the task of testifying to the good news of God's grace" (Acts 20:16 – 24).

Paul went on to say that he would probably never see them again. He declared that he was innocent of the blood of all men. He said he taught them all about the whole counsel of God. Paul warned the elders to watch over their flock because the Holy Spirit made you their shepherd. He reminded them that the church belongs to

Jesus, who purchased it with His blood. Paul said to protect the flock from the wolves that will try to devour them. Also, watch for people within the church who speak perversely and try to draw the disciples away from you and God.

Paul ended by saying that God and His grace would guide them through any trial. For we are all in the ministry for God's glory and for building up the body of Christ because it is more blessed to give than to receive. They all knelt, prayed, and wept with sorrow. The elders walked Paul to the ship and said goodbye. They knew they would never see him on this earth again.

Paul and Luke traveled by sea and made stops at ports in Tyre and Ptolemais before landing in Caesarea to meet with Philip, the evangelist, at his house.

Onward to Jerusalem

Philip told Paul that the people in Jerusalem saw him as an enemy and a traitor because of his teachings "against" the Jewish people, the Law of Moses, and the customs of the temple. He warned Paul that the Jews wanted to kill him in Jerusalem. But, Paul insisted on giving the donations that he collected from the churches to the Jerusalem Christians.

Paul told Philip that he was willing to die in Jerusalem for the sake of the Lord. Philip instructed him to take four Jewish men with him, who had purification rites, pay for their rites, and become purified along with them before going into the temple. This act of redemption would show the Jewish people that Paul was still following their laws and customs.

After seven days of purification, some Asian Jews saw Paul at the temple. Previously, these same men had seen Paul in Jerusalem associating with a Gentile named Trophimus. They assumed that Trophimus was with Paul in the temple. A riot ensued on the temple mount, and a crowd of angry Jews cried out against Paul, "Men of Israel, help! This is the man who is teaching everyone everywhere against the people and the law and this place. Moreover, he even brought Greeks into the temple and has defiled this holy place" (Acts 21:28, ESV).

The crowd falsely accused Paul of desecrating the temple by having a Gentile with him. They dragged Paul out of the temple and violently beat him. A Roman commander, named Lysias, and his soldiers interrupted the riot. When Paul told Lysias that he was a Roman citizen, he turned him over to the Jewish chief priests.

Paul told the chief priests and the members of the Sanhedrin that he was a Pharisee and on trial for having hope in the resurrection of the dead. When he said this, a dispute between the Pharisees and Sadducees broke out, and the council was divided. "The Sadducees say that there is no resurrection, and that there are neither angels nor spirits, but the Pharisees believe all these things" (Acts 23:8). The dispute became violent. They forced Paul into the barracks. That night God told Paul to take courage. He said, *"As you have testified about me in Jerusalem, so you must also testify in Rome"* (Acts 23:11).

The next morning more than forty Jews formed a conspiracy, went to the chief priests and the elders and said, "We have taken a solemn oath not to eat anything until we have killed Paul. [15]Now then, you and the Sanhedrin, petition the commander to bring him before you on the pretext of wanting more accurate information about his case. We are ready to kill him before he gets here" (Acts 23:14 – 15).

After learning of this news, Lysias wrote a letter to the Roman Governor of Judea, Antonius Felix. He explained the accusations against Paul had to do with questions concerning their Law. He said no charges brought against Paul deserved death or imprisonment. Lysias also wrote that he told Paul's accusers to present their case to Felix. Then, Lysias ordered the soldiers to secretly transport Paul and the letter to Caesarea and hand them both over to Felix.

Five days later the high priest, some elders, and a lawyer traveled to Caesarea to present their case against Paul to Governor Felix. They said to Felix, [5]"We have found this man to be a troublemaker, stirring up riots among the Jews all over the world. He is a ringleader of the Nazarene sect [6]and even tried to desecrate the temple; so, we seized him.[7] [8]By examining him yourself you will be able to learn the truth about all these charges we are bringing against him" (Acts 24:5 – 8).

¹⁰"When the governor motioned for him to speak, Paul replied: "I know that for a number of years you have been a judge over this nation; so, I gladly make my defense. ¹¹You can easily verify that no more than twelve days ago I went up to Jerusalem to worship. ¹²My accusers did not find me arguing with anyone at the temple, or stirring up a crowd in the synagogues or anywhere else in the city. ¹³And they cannot prove to you the charges they are now making against me. ¹⁴However, I admit that I worship the God of our ancestors as a follower of the Way, which they call a sect. I believe everything that is in accordance with the Law and that is written in the Prophets, ¹⁵and I have the same hope in God as these men themselves have, that there will be a resurrection of both the righteous and the wicked. ¹⁶So, I strive always to keep my conscience clear before God and man" (Acts 24:10 – 16).

Paul continued, ¹⁷"After an absence of several years, I came to Jerusalem to bring my people gifts for the poor and to present offerings. ¹⁸I was ceremonially clean when they found me in the temple courts doing this. There was no crowd with me, nor was I involved in any disturbance. ¹⁹But there are some Jews from the province of Asia, who ought to be here before you and bring charges if they have anything against me. ²⁰Or these who are here should state what crime they found in me when I stood before the Sanhedrin—²¹unless it was this one thing I shouted as I stood in their presence: '*It is concerning the resurrection of the dead that I am on trial before you today.*'

²²Then Felix, who was well acquainted with the Way, adjourned the proceedings. "When Lysias the commander comes," he said, "I will decide your case." ²³He ordered the centurion to keep Paul under guard but to give him some freedom and permit his friends to take care of his needs" (Acts 24:17 – 23).

²⁴"Several days later Felix came with his wife Drusilla, who was Jewish. He sent for Paul and listened to him as he spoke about faith in Christ Jesus. ²⁵As Paul talked about righteousness, self-control and the judgment to come, Felix was afraid and said, "That's enough for now! You may leave. When I find it convenient, I will send for you."

[26]At the same time, he was hoping that Paul would offer him a bribe, so he sent for him frequently and talked with him. [27]When two years had passed, Governor Felix was succeeded by Porcius Festus, but because Felix wanted to grant a favor to the Jews, he left Paul in prison" (Acts 24:24 – 27).

Paul Appears before Governor Festus (60 A.D.)

[1]"Three days after arriving in the province, Festus went up from Caesarea to Jerusalem, [2]where the chief priests and the Jewish leaders appeared before him and presented the charges against Paul. [3]They requested Festus, as a favor to them, to have Paul transferred to Jerusalem, for they were preparing an ambush to kill him along the way. [4]Festus answered, "Paul is being held at Caesarea, and I myself am going there soon. [5]Let some of your leaders come with me, and if the man has done anything wrong, they can press charges against him there" (Acts 25:1 – 5).

[6]"After spending eight or ten days with them, Festus went down to Caesarea. The next day he convened the court and ordered that Paul be brought before him. [7]When Paul came in, the Jews who had come down from Jerusalem stood around him. They brought many serious charges against him, but they could not prove them" (Acts 25:6 – 7).

[8]"Then Paul made his defense: "I have done nothing wrong against the Jewish law or against the temple or against Caesar." [9]Festus, wishing to do the Jews a favor, said to Paul, "Are you willing to go up to Jerusalem and stand trial before me there on these charges?"

[10]Paul answered: "I am now standing before Caesar's court, where I ought to be tried. I have not done any wrong to the Jews, as you yourself know very well. [11]If, however, I am guilty of doing anything deserving death, I do not refuse to die. But if the charges brought against me by these Jews are not true, no one has the right to hand me over to them. I appeal to Caesar!" [12]After Festus had conferred with his council, he declared: "You have appealed to Caesar. To Caesar (Rome) you will go!" (Acts 25:8 – 12).

NOTES

[1]"When and Why Was Saul's Name Changed to Paul?" *GotQuestions.org,* 7 July 2015, www.gotquestions.org/Saul-Paul.html.

[2]"What Is the Mystery of Faith?" *GotQuestions.org,* 2 Dec. 2014, www.gotquestions.org/mystery-of-faith.html.

[3]"What Does It Mean When Jesus Says, 'My Yoke Is Easy and My Burden Is Light' (Matthew 11:30)?" *GotQuestions.org,* 15 Oct. 2010, www.gotquestions.org/yoke-easy-burden-light.html.

[4]"What Is Sanctification? What Is the Definition of Christian Sanctification?" *GotQuestions.org,* 18 Apr. 2015, www.gotquestions.org/sanctification.html.

[5]"Girls with Swords: How to Carry Your Cross like a Hero." *Girls with Swords: How to Carry Your Cross like a Hero*, by Lisa Bevere, Christian Large Print, 2014, p. 74.

[6]"First 5." Teaching by Joel Muddamalle, and Hannah Schindler, First 5, 7 Apr. 2019, first5.org/plans/Ezra%20Nehemiah/ff_o-o_weekend_5/.

[7]Sprowl, R.C. "Ligonier Ministries The Teaching Fellowship of R.C. Sproul." *Ligonier Ministries,* 7 Apr. 2019, www.ligonier.org/learn/devotionals/making-known-gods-manifold-wisdom/.

[8]Stedman, Ray C. "Message: Hope, Riches, and Power (Ephesians 1:18-23)." *RayStedman.org*, 11 May 2017, www.raystedman.org/new-testament/ephesians/hope-riches-and-power.

[9]Guzik, David. "Ephesians Chapter 6." *Enduring Word*, 23 Aug. 2018, www.enduringword.com/bible-commentary/ephesians-6/.

[10]McGee, Matthew. *Chronology of Apostle Paul's Journeys and Epistles*, 16 May 2017, www.matthewmcgee.org/paultime.html.

[11]"What Is the Passover Lamb?" *GotQuestions.org*, 15 Apr. 2013, www.gotquestions.org/Passover-Lamb.html.

Meet the Author

The author has a bachelor's degree in teaching, a master's degree in counseling, and a doctoral degree in educational leadership. Bridget has worked in education for twenty years and used her research knowledge, counseling, and teaching skills to write this Bible study. She is the director of an advising and career center at a community college and the curriculum designer and instructor of the college's new student orientation course. Comparable to the learning and study strategies that Bridget teaches to freshman, she applied similar concepts and methods to writing this book with the goal of (re) orienting new and returning Christians to the faith. She became interested in this topic after attending one of Dr. Brenda Randle's workshops on *How to Birth your Vision*. Bridget left the seminar inspired to write a Bible study that would provide the biblical principles that *she* needed to know and learn from her own salvation experience. While Bridget uses the Apostle Paul's prison letters to teach the fundamentals of Christianity, she also shares how the thorns in her heart, mind, soul, and flesh kept her in bondage and from living in the freedom and promises of the abundant life.

Made in the USA
Monee, IL
31 May 2020